Sweet and Sour
Cotton Candy Doesn't Melt

While every precaution has been taken in the preparation of this book, the publisher assumes no responsibility for errors or omissions, or for damages resulting from the use of the information contained herein.

SWEET AND SOUR COTTON CANDY DOESN'T MELT

First edition. June 23, 2024.

Copyright © 2024 Yeong Hwan Choi.

ISBN: 979-8224918003

Written by Yeong Hwan Choi.

Table of Contents

Sweet and Sour
Cotton Candy Doesn't Melt

Yeong hwan Choi

Publication | 2024-06-23
Author | Yeong hwan Choi
EMAIL ◈cyhchs12@naver.com
https://.blog.naver.com/cyhchs12

CONTENT

One day, cotton candy in my hand

Episode 1 Two Cotton Candy
1-1 Please
1-2 Sour
1-3 It's sweet

Episode 2 cotton candy which the sky ate
2-1 At the edge of the rainbow bridge
2-2 Please come back

Episode 3 sticky cotton candy
3-1 to taste
3-2 Fragrance
3-3 Forever

Cotton candy never melted.

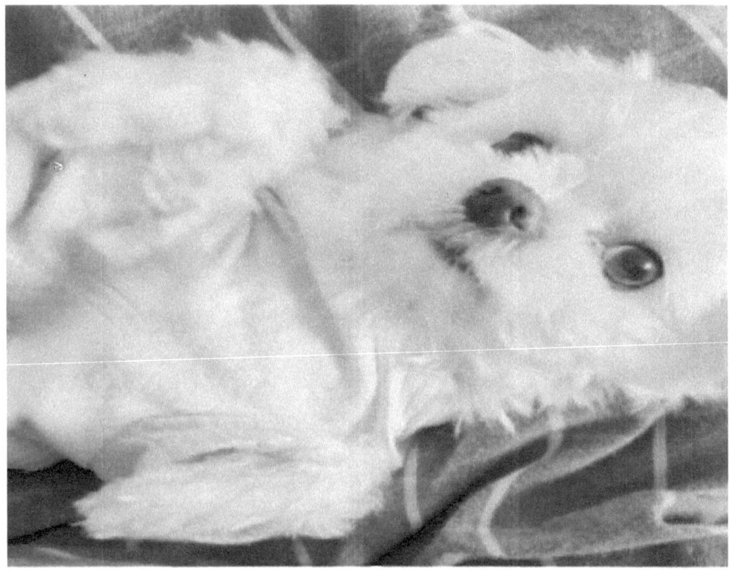

<One day, I got cotton candy in my hand>

When I was a child, my sister and I begged our parents that we wanted to have a dog. My mom was strongly against it, but somehow we found a white cotton candy. The friend who was as sour as his life was the Maltese 'Hope'.

The cotton candy, which was just 40 days old, attracted attention with its snow-white fur, sparkling eyes, and three black beans. It seems like yesterday, but it's been 20 years since we met.

When I was 15 years old, in my second year of middle school, I was on a sunny spring day and on a Saturday. My mother and sister were given cotton balls at a family home. We had another family. After that, they stayed with me for a long time and engraved precious memories in my heart.

The school bell rang. At that time, the concept of "Nolto" was divided into a Saturday off every other week and a Saturday when school was on the way. Mom was waiting in front of the school gate with my younger brother in tow. My mom searched the internet portal 'Yahoo' one week ago without our knowledge, and for some reason she seemed to have changed her mind.

Rumble. That's how I did everything with the angel I met there. Time passed, and when I was about to enter college, the military, a job at a large company, and a civil servant, I met another cotton candy, a lucky one. It wasn't until I was 12 years old that sweet and sour cotton candy with a familiar flavor came to my house. Apparently they were the same Maltese, so they looked and looked somewhat alike, but they didn't have that flavor as much as they were attractive.

The time I spent with Lucky brought me a different kind of happiness, and those were the most precious days for me.

The memories of the old cotton candy were rich in all of my formative years, and her love was indescribable.

However, the moment of separation that came suddenly one day came with an overwhelming sadness. At the age of 17, after the cotton candy went somewhere, I felt the emptiness of the empty place and was filled with nostalgia. Two years later, the second piece of cotton candy disappeared from view at the early age of seven. My heart ached again at the unexpected series of breakups, and it hurt like the sky was about to fall.

As the dark-haired beast experienced two heartbreaking breakups, he realized how much the love left behind by the cotton candy with its white fur inside out meant to him. Finally, a year later, when the great waves in the tsunami stopped and the gentle ripples echoed in my mind, I wrote to make memories with my babies.

Her calm heart throbbed again, and tears welled up in her eyes. 'Hope' and 'Luck' were like shining stars in my life. Did the two cotton candy be blown away by the wind? Or did he turn into a cloud and ascend to the sky? Or did it melt away with the tears and runny nose?

It is a heartwarming story that those who have sent their dogs to each other can relate to, and I want to share their longing and gratitude with them.

Episode 1 Two Cotton Candy

I still remember the first day I met Hope. Fast forward 21 years, and the school scene unfolds before your eyes. In the middle of the classroom was a green chalkboard, and the chalk was contrasted in three colors: white, red, and blue. The chalk eraser was used to shake chin chin powder off the wall every cleaning time, or to make a loud 'whirring~~~' sound. In front of the classroom, there was a Taegukgi flag and a school song written on it, and not to mention the air conditioner, the fan with the cover removed was spinning from side to side. On the left side of the front of the classroom, a fat CRT TV, instead of the current LCD monitor, sits heavily in a yellow cabinet.

As many as 40 students filled the classroom in one class, and 13 classes were buzzing. Beyond the '90s, when only the strong survived, and closer to the 2002 World Cup, it was an unusually hot early summer day when the cicadas began to chirp.

It was CA time on Saturday. At that time, Korea had just changed from a six-day workweek to a five-day work week, and middle school students used to go to school every other Saturday. It ends before lunchtime, and the subjects are organized as group activities, such as movies, soccer, and bowling. On that day, too, in the summer heat, we huddled together in the classroom and watched a movie. The friends huddled in front of the TV, enjoying "Harry Potter and the Sorcerer's Stone."

"Wow, Harry is so cool!" One of my friends yelled.

"That's right, I want to use magic like Harry." Another friend replied.

The hands of the clock ticked to noon, and the sound of Tiri Li Li Li signaled the end of the day with the clamor of the children to see more movies. I trudged through the playground and out of the school gates. For some reason, my mom parked the car on the side of the road and waited for me with my sister. I didn't ask what was going on, I got into the car, but I remember seeing my brother's face unusually bright. It was the first time we went to see cotton candy.

Today, there are a variety of dog breeds, including bichons, schnauzers, bulldogs, huskies, and Pomeranians, but back then it was common for friends to have Yorkshire terriers, Shih Tzu, and occasionally Maltese and poodles. And before you know it, the Maltese suddenly became popular with Koreans and became the number one player in the rankings. We headed to a two-room building that was a 10-minute drive away. Along the way, I had a conversation with my mom and sister.

"Mom, that puppy is so pretty! I can't wait to see you."

"She was very cute in the photo. He looked healthy," Mom replied.

My sister was already busy deciding on a name. "I think 'Hope' would be good. Hope is a beautiful name!"

Upon arrival, a woman in her early 30s opened the door and greeted me. And at the same time, there was a 'poooch' sound. The puppy looked healthy and I remember him as about five years old. She told me that she had given birth to four cubs, and that one had already been delivered. Of the three remaining dogs, only two were going to be given away, so she said she would raise one with her mother.

We drank the juice and couldn't take our eyes off the cubs and their mom. One boy and two girls. Two of the three went under the couch and didn't come out, and one of the only boys came to us and flirted with us, but our family wanted a female. I'm also a man, so I like princesses for animals. Meanwhile, a girl under the couch started licking over the juice cups that my sister and I were drinking. It was so adorable, we all burst out laughing.

"Do you like him?" she asked cautiously.

She seemed to have already lost her heart for the baby. "yes, I like him. It's so cute," he said, slowly approaching our cautiously outstretched hand and sniffing it. In that moment, I felt a special connection to her. A small, white-haired cotton candy. His eyes were a mixture of curiosity and fear.

We decided to get the puppy. When she tried to take her away, the mother puppy followed her to the door and stared at her daughter endlessly. Will the heart of a mother who struggles twice be crushed? It was salty for nothing.

The younger sister saw the sad look in the mother's eyes, and then cautiously approached the mother and said to her:

"It's okay, I'll take care of your baby. Don't worry too much, my family will love you very much."

The younger sister comforted the mother puppy by gently stroking her head. The mother looked at her sister with sad eyes and wagged her tail slightly. His eyes were always sad, but he seemed a little relieved by the warm comfort. As she walked out the door, she kept looking back and waving to her mother. The mother just watched her daughter leave.

I wonder if the cotton candy in the car will melt in the hot weather. I turned on the air conditioner right away, but the weather was so bad that I stuck my tongue out. Even the way she looked was so adorable, but she didn't seem to know how to say goodbye to her mother yet. My family, who are raising dogs for the first time, brought in a small piece of cotton, but just in case, we prepared a soft cushion in a fairly large box.

Hope curled up inside, looking around. Mom got behind the wheel and occasionally looked back to talk to Hope.

"Hope, our house is yours now. I'll love you a lot."

Hope tilted her head in response to her mother's voice. The sun was shining through the window, and the trees were dyed green. Occasionally the leaves rustled in the breeze passing by, and before I knew it, she was sitting on my lap and looking at the scenery curiously. The little sister gently touched the angel's little feet and smiled. "Hope is our family now. I love you a lot, and I need you to take good care of me."

As soon as we got home, we were excited to welcome our new family. Cotton candy looked around with her small body, and then curled up in a tired little body and fell asleep. My mom, my sister, and I watched silently.

"She's like an angel. I'll get you a cushion," my sister whispered.

Mom smiled as she listened to Hope's small breathing.

"What a beautiful baby."

While I slept on the soft cushions, I bought a lot of extra items on the internet as if it were my first time raising a puppy. A small bed, a soft blanket, a variety of toys, bath products, and even food.

My dad got home from work. As soon as I opened the door, I entered the living room and smiled brightly at Hope.

"Oh, a pretty angel has come to our house!" said Dad.

"Dad, this child's name is Hope. It's so cute, isn't it?" she said. Dad gently stroked the little head of Hope who had gone to dreamland.

"It's really cute. Let's take care of it."

But on the first night, Cotton Candy started crying all night. "Whimper, whin," she cried, as if calling out to her mother in a small voice, and the whole family was heartbroken. I brought her to my room and carefully laid her down on the soft cushions I had prepared next to her bed so that she could calm down.

The crying didn't stop in my room. "Whimper," I couldn't help but see my tiny body trembling. He held out his hand and stroked his white fur and whispered. "Hope, it's okay. I'm going to sleep here."

Eventually, I stayed up all night watching her. When she stopped crying with the soft, warm sound of her breathing, she would doze off for a while, but as soon as she started crying again, she would wake up. Somehow, the first night passed, and the morning light came in through the window.

Everyone in the family smiled as they recounted their first night with Hope. "It's been a lot of work," Mom said.

"Hope will adjust soon," Dad added.

At that time, South Korea was just beginning to establish its pet culture. Compared to the way dogs are raised in Western Europe or North America, we were clumsy and lacking. And people's awareness wasn't deep.

At that time, Korea was growing rapidly and moving towards becoming a developed country, but there was a lack of information and awareness about animals as well as pet dogs. A time of barbarism, shall we?

Although the animal protection laws are still poor in Korea, at that time, dyed chicks, turtles, and birds were sold in front of schools, and people put living hamsters and crayfish in the claw machines and put coins as if they were entertaining. And without proper information, out of curiosity and fun, they raised various creatures, and often died on the way, but now that I think about it, I was really ignorant and ignorant. In the same way, like other children my age, I raised chicks, birds, and hamsters, and I kept grasshoppers in dragonflies and square plastic containers. It was a time when they caught grasshoppers, dragonflies, and cicadas. "I'm eating chili peppers.... Soothe and eat...

While looking for cicadas, a lady from the next neighborhood said on the porch, "I caught a cicada here, so take it!" There was a time when I was yelling. In the early 2000s, the doors were open, and neighbors came and went frequently. Perhaps because of this, there was a lot of affection between human beings.

The world has changed a lot now. The love of humanity has disappeared and the awareness of animals and living things has increased somewhat. That's how important it is to change social perceptions. Having killed so many lives when I was young, I am ashamed of my ignorance, and sometimes I miss the days of innocence. Now, in the midst of these changes, I feel that my life is getting deeper as I get older.

After all, dogs in those days were no exception. It was a time when people in the countryside still kept them outside with a pretty thick rope around their necks. It was our first time getting a dog, so we didn't have enough of it.

In addition to online purchases, when I went to the supermarket to buy something for cotton candy, I bought a toilet box with a structure like a cage. The baby's poop and urine dripped to the bottom. Now that I think about it, it was a very incongruous thing for that cute creature. Of course, Hope never once stepped inside a prison-like cage. The automatic waterer, which comes out only when the water is licked with the tongue, is stuck in the shed for life.

I also bought too much baby food. At first, it had no teeth, so it was soaked in water and dissolved like baby food. And it seems that the toys I bought were not suitable for teeth grinding. That's why he would bite our socks after school.

The sight of cotton candy running around with its socks in its twitching steps was so cute. As time went on, it became more and more active. Especially when the teeth grinding period came, I remember browsing around the house and tickling the corner wallpaper or on my head and biting my hair.

One day I found a white baby tooth in my sock that was being bitten by a cotton candy that looked like a small wild animal. "Mommy, hope has lost its teeth!" I exclaimed, and she smiled. "I'm becoming an adult now."

After the baby teeth fell out, the adult dog's teeth were reborn, but the habit of biting things continued until he became an old dog. We used to take him to the vet regularly to keep him healthy. In particular, he visited frequently to get a heartworm shot.

There were two veterinary clinics near my home. One side was run by a male veterinarian, and although the hospital looked a bit messy, he had the reputation of graduating from Seoul National University. On the other hand, the other was a hospital run by a female veterinarian, and it was always neat and the equipment was kept clean.

Since Korea is a nation that dies and dies when it comes to Seoul National University, we used to go to hospitals with male veterinarians because of our fame, but gradually we changed our direction to hospitals run by female veterinarians.

"It's really nice and clean here," Mom said. "Hope seems to be more comfortable."

There, she took care of her and received the necessary vaccinations and treatment.

However, on my second visit to the hospital, I became extremely sensitive when I saw the sharp needle of the syringe. His little body trembled, and he struggled to get away from the vet. Even though the needle didn't touch my skin, I whined loudly and snuggled. Seeing this, the vet put the medicine in my sister's hand. She flinched as she took the medicine in her hand and carefully applied it to the back of her neck, but then she calmed down as if relieved by the warm touch.

We bought another one. Another small bed was soft and cozy, and the toys came in different colors and shapes to match the teething. But for some reason, it didn't suit my taste in cotton candy. Hope was more interested in everyday human use than in the things we bought.

I also bought a variety of bath products. I chose a shampoo and conditioner that fits my little body. My first bath was like a war. After filling the tub with lukewarm water, she gently lifted the baby up. Perhaps he didn't want to dissolve in water like cotton candy, so he kept lifting his front paws and twisting his body. Every time the little paw struggled, water splashed in all directions, and I carefully supported the baby with my hand so as not to hurt him. And I was afraid that the foam would get on my face, so I applied shampoo to my body. She held her with one hand and washed off the foam with the other, telling herself, "It's okay, it'll be over soon." She carefully rinsed her face to avoid foaming, and finally wrapped a soft towel around her and hugged her. I looked at the dirty bathroom and felt that it wasn't as easy as I thought. However, there was one final checkpoint. Nowadays, there are many machines that dry the hair because the product is so good, but I even dried the hair with a blow dryer.

The sound of the dryer did not seem easy for a child with a developed sense of hearing. She carefully turned on the blow dryer and let it blow air, but the cotton candy was startled by the noise, twisting her body and trying to avoid the wind. He tried to push the dryer away with his front paws and stepped back. Whenever the blow dryer touched him, he threw back his ears and closed his eyes tightly, turning his head. He soothed Hope with one hand and said quietly, "It's okay, it's over soon," but the final showdown with the dryer was still not over. When his fur was finally dry, he turned to me with a puzzled look on his face, as if he had finished the hard fight. He held the dried cotton candy in his arms and gently stroked it, praising it as "Well done, Hope." Finally, she brushed her fur with a soft comb.

"Hope is so beautiful after taking a bath," she said.

My first walk in the park was also an unforgettable moment. That day, the white cotton candy met the green grass and trees for the first time. He was small, but his eyes and movements were full of enthusiasm. He seemed to be curious about the smells in the scenery that he had never seen before, wondering if he was afraid of the outside world.

When they reached the grass, they began to run around excitedly, as if they had been waiting for them. Sometimes, I couldn't control my energy and didn't even know if I was running around or rolling. He fell down several times, but quickly got up and ran again. It was so adorable and made everyone who saw it while walking around smile.

Cotton candy was taken care of by its owner, who often met its mother puppy when she was out for a walk. The mother puppy ran with longing and relief in her eyes. The baby wagged her tail as if she recognized her mother, and her mother licked her ears. Then the look in his eyes changed. Was it an expression of joy and relief, as if he had met his lost child again?

On my way home from school, cotton candy always greeted me. When I opened the door, the first thing to run up to, twirl its tail like a helicopter, and greet me violently was enough to forget the tiredness of the day. And he was a friend who listened to many stories. I told him what happened at school, how I fought with my friends, what I was happy about and how sad I was. Then, three black beans on white cotton would comfort me and stay with me day and night.

Hope, who found quite a bit of time, naturally blended into her daily life. When I was in high school, mathematical formulas and English words crammed on the blackboard awaited me, and my days were busy with supplementary classes and forced self-study at night. Seeing the moon on the way home in the morning and on the way home late at night, I was able to realize how hot the education fever is in Korea. When I took the SAT and went to university, I started living out of town. I lived in a dormitory during the week and could only go home on weekends. The university campus boasted the beauty of the buildings in harmony with nature, with cherry blossoms in full bloom in spring and autumn leaves in deep color. There was a large pond in the center of the campus, surrounded by a green lawn and the historic brick Central Library building.

The first year of college was a time of freedom. As a freshman and a newcomer, I spent my days drinking with friends, going to karaoke, and making a girlfriend for the first time. One evening after midterms, we went to Hope's house.

"How long are you going to make me dance on your shoulders!" one of my friends exclaimed, "Baskin Robbins Surrey One!" He shouted and shook his shoulders.

"1,2,3.... 31", "Drink, drink~" Everyone laughed and shouted. As the game progressed, the shoulder dance became more and more intense.

"Bani Bunny Bani Bani Bani~" Another friend started playing "Bunny Bunny". The game was getting hotter and hotter, and we were intoxicated by the endless laughter.

After the drinking game, we moved to the karaoke bar. A friend of mine started dancing with enthusiasm to "Girls' Generation's 'Gee'."

"Gee, Gee, Gee, Gee, Baby, Baby, Baby~" The friends sang and danced along with their friends. It was filled with scorching heat, like a small concert hall. At that moment, I mustered up the courage to speak to her sitting next to me.

"I've got something to tell you," she said, her voice trembling, but she smiled at me.

"What do you mean?" her eyes twinkled.

"Actually, I like you. Do you want to go out with us?" She hesitated for a moment, but then replied with a bright smile.

"I like you too. Let's go out together!" she replied. That's how we confirmed our feelings for each other, and our first relationship full of excitement began.

That night, a new love came amid the excitement of karaoke and the support of friends, and precious memories with friends were also combined. And every weekend when I came home, Hope was still waiting for me. "Hope, it's been a while!" he happily shouted, "General Hope!" I hugged him. However, I gradually spent less and less time with cotton candy, which made me feel bitter in my heart.

Before I was in my second year, I joined the Army like any able-bodied man.

"Loyalty!" we shouted every morning as boot camp life began.

"We are the Republic of Korea Army, loyal to our country and our people. One. We will defend liberal democracy and become a force for the reunification of the country. Second, we become victors in ground wars through training like real battles. We obey the law and obey the orders of our superiors. Fourth, we are firmly united in brotherhood and honor and fidelity."

Training lasted from early in the morning until late in the evening. Everything was a routine, a routine that was repeated every day. One day, while I was resting after training, I received a letter from my parents. When I opened the envelope, I found a picture of cotton candy inside. In the photo, she was looking at me with a loving expression.

"Is it your dog?" asked a comrade who was reading the letter with him.

"Yes, it's our dog. Hope," I said, showing him the picture.

"It's so cute. I also have a cat at home, and I miss it," he said, expressing his longing for his pet.

That night, before I went to bed, I pulled out the cotton candy picture again. Then I remembered the time we had spent together. I missed going for walks, playing with her, and playing with her.

In a letter, my parents told me that the white angel was doing well. She told me that she misses me too, and that she often goes into the room I used to use and waits for me.

"Hope, I miss you so much. I can't wait to go on vacation and go for a walk with you again," I said to myself as I fell asleep.

When I finally completed the boot camp and was assigned to my own unit, I was able to call home once a week when I was a private second class. The sound of "Boom!" over the phone reminded me of the warmth of home. This time, "Kigging Kie!" The voice looking for me reminded me of my nostalgic home. When I became a corporal, I was able to speak freely on the phone, and because of that, I was able to talk to Hope often. Every time I came home from vacation, the reaction of cotton candy was the same. "Hope, my brother is here! How are you? Our General!" made me forget the hardships of military life for a while.

His green uniform felt heavy, and the floor of the training camp was infinitely cold compared to his parents' house. But time passes anyway. Now I could read the anticipation and respect in the eyes of my successors as they looked at me.

Finally, the day has come. During the break after lunch, I sat around a bench surrounded by vines in front of the PX, chatting with several of my successors. The recruits who had just arrived in their battalion as second class soldiers in training were curious about their future military life and asked me to tell them about my experiences. "Sergeant Choi, no now! What was it like when you first came in?" one of the writers asked.

"At first, I was scared of everything. But over time, I got used to it. The difficulties you are going through now will pass."

After completing the discharge report, I was encouraged and applauded by the company commander, and on the way from the barracks to the guardhouse, my juniors were standing in a line looking at me. There was regret and remembrance in their eyes. With every step, the voices of his successors echoed.

"Loyalty!" shouted his closest successor, saluting.

"Thank you for your hard work. Hurry up and find a girlfriend in society and fight!" shouted my successor, who was not much different from me.

"I love you. Thank you, comrades-in-arms. Comrades-in-arms!!" Finally, one of the juniors blurted out a half-joke, half-serious talk. Finally, the voices of "loyalty" came together as one, and I bowed my head and smiled at them.

As he passed the guardhouse, he had a big smile on his face, but there was also a sense of loneliness in his heart. The feeling of freedom and liberation I had hoped for was not always joyful. The view from inside was one I had become accustomed to over the past two years.

After returning to school, taking a fourth-year job hunting class and getting a job at a large company, my meetings with Hope were reduced to once or twice a month. I was very happy when I applied and received the acceptance notice, but I was excited about the anticipation of meeting Hope on the day I went to my parents' house despite my busy life in Seoul. "Hope, I'm here!" he said, running around the living room when he opened the door, unable to see his legs.

The way back to Seoul was disappointing every time. At half past five in the morning, the alarm went off in the apartment. "Ding ding ding ding~" Samsung's unique wake-up trumpet rang out in full.

"It's starting again. Let's go do morning gymnastics..." I rubbed my tired eyes and got up and said to myself:

The site of a large corporation construction company was a higher version of the military. I majored in civil engineering and was lucky enough to be in charge of a large construction site in Seoul. But it wasn't comfortable. On the contrary, as large-scale construction was carried out in the middle of the city, they suffered from a lot of dust, noise complaints, and stress. Along with grueling meetings throughout the day, there were safety concerns, scheduling, and unforeseen emergencies. The huge cranes at the construction site were busy, and rebar, concrete, and asphalt were transported non-stop. Day after day passed amid huge pieces of equipment, roaring, and dust.

Morning gymnastics was for day laborers and all workers who came to work at 6 a.m. Under the standards of the Safe Labor Act, it is an act of warming up for a safety accident by announcing the start of the day. All the staff gathered together to stretch together and do simple gymnastics to prepare for the day. "Shhh After gymnastics, I went straight to work after breakfast. During the meeting, they reviewed the day's work plan and confirmed the tasks assigned to each team. I mostly went around the site, checking the progress of the work, and running around to find a quick solution when a problem arose.

Some days, I held up a blueprint and discussed the construction method with the rebar manager. In the midst of my daily routine, I suddenly began to feel that my values and life here did not match. "I don't have time at all. Is this really inhabited?"

The salary at a large company was really high, and I got along well with my colleagues, but in the end, I said goodbye to the construction company I had worked for for two years. Then he went home and prepared for the civil service exam. At that time, the popularity of the official skyrocketed. On the 9 o'clock news, the words "Noryangjin" and "Cupbap" appeared almost every day. It is said to be a holy place for students preparing for the civil service examination, and young people flock to it. Lined with cram schools, high school districts, and shops offering cheap food, the place was bustling with activity day and night. In the news, it was reported every day that the competition rate in the civil service exam often exceeded 100 to 1. According to a survey, more young people want to become civil servants than big companies. Even talented people who graduated from Seoul National University said that they would challenge the civil service exam. Perhaps it was a reflection of the trend of emphasizing stability and work-life balance regardless of academic background, but in the evening, Noryangjin became more lively. The cram school and study room, where the lights did not go out until late in the day, aroused sadness on the one hand, and enthusiasm on the other. Their appearance was a good illustration of the social craze of the time.

On the other hand, I was able to spend a lot of time with cotton candy when I came home. At midnight, when everyone in the family was asleep, Hope would go to each of our rooms to say hello, and when the day came, she would wake us up before us, scratching our blankets with her little paws. Rubbing my sleepy eyes, I wake up and hope greets me with a wagging tail. I kissed him on the nose.

Breathing in the morning air and taking a walk around the neighborhood together energized me when I was studying. Even though it was a walk every time I went out, I looked around, sniffed it intently, marked it, and followed me with small steps. The walk was a precious time for the two of us, and we were able to start the day feeling each other's presence

Hope has always been with me like a shadow in my daily life. In the evenings, we forgot about sweets together and spent time watching TV at the same time. At such times, he liked to sit on my lap and be still. Feeling the warmth and soft fur, I felt comfortable too.

She has always been a precious and special presence in my life. It made my life richer, but at the time, I was deceived by familiarity and didn't always appreciate the time. Through all this time, it was not just a part of the family, it was a part of life. The hardship of going to school early in the morning and coming home at 11 p.m., the excitement and familiarity of living abroad in college, the hardship of military life, and the stress of work were all together.

(40-day-old sweet cotton candy)

1-1 Please

In autumn, when a chilly wind was blowing under a clear sky, I was working hard to study in the reading room in order to change jobs in the civil service at a large company. I was 27 and Cotton Candy was 12.

And we were excited to welcome our new family. I can't forget my first encounter with another cotton candy. The little Maltese had a gentle and kind look in his button-like eyes. Looking at Lucky Yi who exuded a different energy than Hope, I felt that another special relationship was approaching.

When her mother noticed that Hope was getting older and not as active as she used to be, she asked, "Doesn't Hope look too lonely?" He said. I sympathized with her, saying, "Yes. It would be nice if Hope had a friend." I replied.

There was also a desire to put lively sweet cotton candy on top of the sweet and sour cotton candy. My father said, "Hope was so active at first, but now that she's older, she's calmed down. If you're lucky enough to have a baby, the atmosphere in your home will be a little more lively." He said. Everyone in the family agreed to welcome a new family.

Sister: "What is the name of the second child? I wish it was a meaningful name like Hope..."

Mom: "yes, it should be a meaningful name. Hope has always brought hope to our family. I want my new dog to have that name."

Dad: "yes, it would be nice to have a name that brings joy and happiness to everyone. What do you think the name "luck" is? It's like luck has come to my house."

Sister: "Lucky...Great! I think the name luck is full of good things."

Mother: "Hope and good luck, just hearing the name makes me feel good."

Sister: "Then you decide! From now on, you're in luck. But can I be called Uni?"

Dad: "Well, Wooni is cute and easy to call. If you're a family member, you can call him 'Ooni.'"

Mother: "Yes, Ooni."

Sister: "All right, Unija. Let's be happy together!"

In this way, the new puppy was named Lucky, and the whole family would call him "Ooni" for short. Sadly, at the time, the perception of puppy mills was not widely known in Korea. And I realized too late that the age difference wasn't necessarily good for Hope.

Lucky was a puppy from a dog center, not a foster home. At that time, the culture of dog adoption was much worse than it is now, and many puppies were born in unhygienic and inhumane conditions.

After checking the baby through the glass of the shop, when I entered the dog center, I saw her living inside a narrow transparent wall. Among them, the cotton candy that stood out was the 'uni'. Moth wagged his tail energetically in the space, attracting our attention. The dog center's foster care officer showed me the lucky one and gave me a brief explanation of his health. Looking into their bright eyes, she imagined the days she would spend with this little creature. As I walked home with my arms in my arms, I felt a heavy sense of responsibility as well as joy.

When she arrived home, she reacted sensitively to unfamiliar smells and creatures. Lucky was carefully placed on the floor, and Hope watched him with a wary look. Lucky didn't care about Hope's reaction, and began to run around the house innocently.

The sour cotton candy that had been watching her like that acted like a mother. Suddenly, when the sweet cotton candy cried in a low voice, it rushed over and circled around it. He didn't leave his side, as if to protect a body smaller than himself.

"Uh-huh," he cried out in a low voice, and even as he was eating, he would come up to him, sniff it, and lean close to it. Thinking it was a cub, the female's instinct to keep approaching and protecting it seemed to kick in. Then, as I held him in my arms, the sweet and sour cotton candy was ready.

"Lucky, do you know how much Hope cares for you?" she laughed happily at their actions. And the first encounter of sweet and sour cotton candy is preserved on my cell phone video.

I gently hugged them. Uni was bewildered by the environment at home, which she had never seen before, but she soon felt comfortable in her arms. His warmth and soft fur made him feel like Hope had reunited with his babyhood. Uni looked around for a moment, then quickly fell asleep. After that first night, they slowly grew accustomed to each other. As time passed, however, it became less desirable to bring a new angel to the elder son.

Hope was stressed out as Ooni grew up little by little. As he began to gnash his teeth and entered adolescence, assertive, he sought to protect his space more and more, and sometimes seemed tired of his youthful enthusiasm and vigorous behavior.

Her mother said, "Hope doesn't play as well as she used to. Maybe we've stressed them out?" He was worried, and I nodded in agreement.

On my way to buy baby kaka, I stopped at a dog center. It was a time when people didn't come, so I think the owner was caught off guard. It was really shocking when the big tent was pulled up behind the dog center. More than 20 puppies were seen giving birth in cramped cages.

I had a conversation with the owner of an unscrupulous dog center.

The proprietor said, "We can't do anything about it to survive," and I was furious. It was really unbearable for humans to exploit not only humans but also animals for money by taking advantage of their relative weakness. For these people, dogs were just a way to make money. The attitude of the owner of the dog center gave me a deep skepticism about human nature. As I watched the mothers of puppies who spent their entire lives in cages to give birth to puppies, I couldn't help but think of the despair and pain they felt.

'Is this really something I have to do in order to make a living?' After the age of 30, when there was a big change in relationships, I hated the dark-haired beasts even more. It wasn't bad to just be independent of people and be alone, and I was happy. In South Korea, animal cruelty and the disposal of young lives in garbage bags still occur frequently. And the level of punishment that is a legal sanction is weak. How can we bully the weak to confirm their existence and achieve their goals? Isn't that cowardly?

She brought her there, but she couldn't forget the puppies and their mothers. It was a pity that some of the babies on display were not sold, leaving them in cages in the darkness and giving birth to their babies. Even when the baby moved there, the mothers were very young. In such an environment, neither mother nor child could be healthy. I was also worried about the health of the lucky man who received such an inheritance. If the offspring born in such an environment are healthy, how healthy would they be?

I don't see people who take advantage of the weak as human beings. These feelings deepened as I grew older. In my social life, I have often seen the dark side of human nature, and I have realized many times how useless human relationships are. On the other hand, as I grew up Hope and Luck, I learned that animals don't betray them. The two cotton candy, united by innocence and loyalty, were more precious than anyone else.

(The sweet cotton candy that took away sister's cushion)

1-2 Sour

Hope was the first of the dignified and dignified. And in our patriarchal house, he was the best to follow his father, and he knew his order so well that when he came in after work, he would wag his tail and run faster than anyone else.

The sour cotton candy that Daddy wished for was generally wide-eyed, and his eyes seemed to be talking to him. Her white fur is semi-curly, so when she strokes it, she often gets tangled in her fingertips. Her pink belly was as soft as the delicate petals, and her tail was always active. And, unlike the Maltese's weak kneecaps, they were very strong and healthy. Even three black beans were always shiny, and the jelly soles that couldn't be stopped once touched were like legal drugs. Except for the occasional reddish fur from sucking his feet, he was generally neat.

When I held it, I felt a 'little squirrel' and it was even more adorable. The legs were shorter than I expected, but they were rather cute. In fact, she looked more like a dignified general than a princess.

Like the father lion holding a baby lion on a cliff in The Lion King, when I wrapped my hands around Hope and raised it to the sky, I was overwhelmed with emotion. It was that strong, and I thought all the puppies were healthy.

Due to his excellent immunity, he has been healthy for 17 years without any major illnesses. And while small dogs are said to have hip and kneecap problems, a walk of about 30 minutes is appropriate, but Hope often goes over an hour. Thirty minutes was too short a time for the great general.

The route of running over the asphalt parking lot, passing through the sand of the playground, and then going around the perimeter path to the park was a familiar route for us.

His walking style was unstubborn, and he followed me wherever I went. And she loved to sniff around on walks. I passed among the cars in the parking lot of my apartment, sniffing them one by one. When I reached the playground, I pressed my nose against the sand and enjoyed the new smells here and there. As I circled the trail, my nose kept busy, noticing the green grass, trees, and the tracks of other dogs. The tail waged incessantly, and the small body did not stand still for a moment, expressing happiness. He was always running around energetically and reading the world in his own way.

When I go to my regular checkups, I think, "I've never seen someone so healthy. You must have very good genes. Is it the power of home breeding? "It's rare to find a Maltese so healthy at this age. It's amazing." The vet would be impressed.

Every time I heard that, I thought to myself: 'Hope was such a special puppy. Is it because of good genes and family upbringing? Or is it because we feel how much we love and care for Hope?'

Hope looked at us with those sparkling eyes every time she heard the vet's compliments. However, behind this exterior, there was also a characteristic Maltese sword. He exuded a personality that is often referred to as a "devil dog" on YouTube. He had a confident personality, and when he was bothered or didn't like himself, he would say "Roar!" with a small but strong cry. The sound of the motorcycle starting, along with the sour cotton candy, was indeed sour.

'Maltese won't put up with it'

The 'growl' that came out of its small mouth was more of a lethal attraction than a threat, and sometimes it was so amusing that it was deliberately irritating. It was so ferocious that you could only touch it with ski gloves. He had a strong ego and was open about his demands.

His bowel habits were also unique. When he was in a bad mood, he would lose his temper on purpose and and pee on the blanket or carpet other than the pad. On days when the whole family went out or my dad wasn't around, I was unusually cocky. On days like this, I waited for my dad at the front door with a shoe rack.

There was a peculiar way of playing with the devil dog. When I played the game "Coco Coco Coco Mouth!" or "Rice Barley Rice Rice Barley Barley," I would growl and then I couldn't stand it and gave a "hook" bite.

He stroked the soft fur and blew a breeze into the hair. "Huh—" The wind shook Hope's fur slightly.

"Meng?" he asked, tilting his head and looking at me.

I turned my head away as if nothing had happened, and the cotton candy stared at me for a moment before lowering its head back to my lap. Once again, "Huh—" I blew in. Once again, he turned his head to look up at me, but again I pretended not to notice. Cotton candy looked at me with a puzzled look, but this time she didn't turn her head. I blew again, as if I had been waiting. "Hoo-ahh I couldn't hold back my laughter and laughed out loud. Then Cotton Candy paused for a moment and looked at me. It's like, 'What's wrong? Stop!' My heart melted at the cute reaction that seemed to say.

"Okay, okay. I'm not going to do it anymore. Come on~"

"Knock down!" "Knock down!" he shouted as he circled the living room and entered the master bedroom. When I called him "come here", he was like a cat with a chic that never came. He glanced at me, his drooping ears moving slightly, and then turned away. He would usually find something to do and go to the fridge, or sit on a cushion and look out the window.

Her sister said, "Come here," but Hope didn't even blink. On the other hand, when my dad said, "Hope, come here," I immediately ran. It was infinitely weaker for the first in seniority.

Even after I went through puberty, I would be even less talkative. Now I had to go looking for my owner myself, touching the soft white fur and the soft jelly on the soles of my feet, and sometimes when I heard my footsteps, I would 'scurry' under the couch or under the table, where I couldn't reach them.

Even if I bought him toys, he didn't play much, and he mostly enjoyed interacting with people. When I was bored, I sat down on my family's belly and lay down. He also acted as if he knew himself as a person.

When she looked in the mirror, she didn't show any reaction, and I wondered if she was really human. Unlike the usual puppies that bark or show curiosity when they see themselves in the mirror, Cotton Candy ignored whether they didn't recognize themselves in the mirror. Although she is a cotton candy who is very independent, she liked to sleep between her family's legs or next to her body. When I looked at the cotton candy that made a sleepy 'gurgling' sound, I could tell that I was dreaming a sweet dream.

She was always on the lookout for new things and strangers. When a family brought a new item into the house, they were the first to approach it. As soon as I opened the plastic bag, I stuck my nose in it, sniffed it, and inspected it thoroughly. Sometimes he stuck his nose in and remained motionless for several minutes. Then, with a rustling sound, he took out the object, and checked it carefully. Only then would I step back to see if I was relieved.

The little crab even offered itself as the house's guard dog. It was the same when a stranger came to your home. When the door opened and a stranger entered, I was on my guard. There was a loud 'moon moon moon' sound and a close sniff at the visitors' feet as they circled around. Gradually, I let my guard down and climbed into his lap like a member of the family.

She was the 'Queen of Gluttony'. They didn't eat, and when it was time to eat, they would appear out of nowhere and try to get what people were eating. I didn't give him salty and spicy Korean food because it wasn't good for his health, but my dad would often share human food. As a result, if you didn't brush your teeth regularly, tartar would accumulate. My mom and I often had worrying conversations.

"I haven't eaten in days. You even got a yellow toe. It's because my dad keeps giving me food that people eat," Mom sighed as she looked at Hope.

There was a growl in his hungry stomach, but he put his mouth to the bowl of water instead of food. He gulped down the water but didn't seem to pay any attention to the food.

"Hope, this is really not getting well," I said, stroking my tail.

However, when the night came, when neither mice nor birds knew, things changed a little. It was quiet inside and outside the house, and when everyone was asleep, I heard the sound of agjak aggak in the kitchen. I cautiously lifted my heels and made my way to the kitchen. There he was secretly eating food. It was so cute and sad that it seemed to ease my worries a little. He's very stubborn, but even that was adorable.

I was particularly fond of apples. When he took out an apple, his big eyes sparkled and he wagged his tail gently as he approached his side. When I gave him the whole thing, he didn't touch his mouth, and his round eyes widened even more, and he gave me a look that said, "Please cut it off." If you cut it into small pieces, the sound of chewing will spread throughout the house. Sometimes, when I tried to sneak out a late-night snack at night, I immediately smelled it and knew it like a ghost and ran to it. He used to eat mostly sausage buns and hard-boiled eggs, and his little nose didn't miss any aroma. Scratched the door. I finally had no choice but to open the door, and Hope wagged her tail as she walked into the room and looked at the food she was eating. Then, when I give you a bite, I happily say 'yum yum' 'om nyom nym'

Sometimes, there were days when they gave me meat. He turned into another dog, running around the living room like crazy. "Wow! Wow!" and as they flew around after the fish, it was like watching little Tom and Jerry chase on the spot. If he moved to one side with the meat, he would run in that direction like the wind. Finally, when he put the meat in his mouth, he rushed to the cushion with a proud expression as if he had caught a big game. As if a small bomb had exploded, his energetic and energetic appearance was the same when he ordered the chicken.

When I heard the phone call, I went straight to the front door. It still makes me smile when I think about it.

"Hello, yes, please deliver a chicken. Pride. The address is..." Just hearing the phone call made me whin, wondering if I was already excited.

"Yes, additional sauce," he said, and as the call continued, he couldn't stand it and jumped up to the front door. It was cute to see him waiting in front of the door, wagging his tail gently, just as he had ordered. His tongue was half-sticking out and he continued to stare at the door, looking expectant. Sometimes he would get up and knock on the door, but he would tilt his head and look back.

"I see. So, be careful with the delivery. Thank you," he said, and when he ended the call, he became even more active, as if the chicken had already arrived. Just by the tone of our voices, he knew that his favorite delivery food was coming. In the short time it took for the food to arrive, I went back and forth to the front door several times. Even if I put him on the bed to stay still, when the bell rang, he would use superhuman strength to land lightly on the ground. It was about 80 centimeters tall. Every time the delivery came, Hope jumped upside down at the smell of the chicken, and she was surprised every time.

"Hey, you're amazing!" she said, glancing at me casually and immediately scratching her arm for the chicken.

At that time, our house was a condominium that was completed in '95. The apartment, which was built by Taeyoung Construction, was close to a kindergarten, a municipal art museum, and an arboretum. In addition, the commercial area was developed, and there were many amenities. Green spaces and residential and commercial areas blend well, and they have been together for most of their lives. The complex has a large promenade and well-maintained garden, making it a great place to enjoy cotton candy and strolls. Shops such as E-Mart, Homeplus, and department stores, where I used to walk with my family every weekend, added convenience to my life.

The memories of the '90s and 2000s with Hope were truly precious. When I was a kid, I used to ride roller braid and scooters around the neighborhood. I used to spend time competing in mini-cars on a small track in front of the stationery, and when I sat in front of an arcade machine that was operated with a stick with a 100-won coin, Hope would quietly watch me from the sidelines. We were together when we went to the comic bookstore, playing with Alba at the counter while I was choosing a book, or waiting in the corner looking out.

In the 2000s, digital devices became more and more embedded in our lives. Back in the days when I used to listen to music on Japanese MP3 players and take pictures with digital cameras, there was always a big smile on my SD card.

My mom graduated with a degree in English literature and tutored. Her mother's knee, which was second in rank after her father, was her favorite place. When my mom was teaching English to my students, she sat quietly on her lap, and her eyes moved with her as she explained what she was teaching with her hands.

I left the army and returned to my second year of university. And I was busy with my civil engineering majors. Epidemiology classes were particularly tough. I was tired of studying for assignments and exams every day. It was my little comfort to stay in the dormitory during the week and come home on the weekends to see Hope. When I sat down at my desk to study, Hope would come over to bite my pen. He smiled at Cotton Candy's mischievous behavior.

In the middle of the freedom and busyness of college life, I met my girlfriend a lot. Hope seemed jealous of that, and sometimes when my girlfriend came home, she would come between me and my girlfriend. As if he were the protagonist, when his girlfriend tried to get close to me, he pushed her away with his front paws.

I matured through the hardships of college life, the love of cotton candy, and the tender times with my girlfriend. The time I spent with Hope enriched my college life, and the scenery around my apartment with my family remains a precious memory for me.

They were always with us in our daily lives. In particular, I had a lot of memories with my dad, whose hobbies were hiking and taking pictures, and cotton candy followed me to various places and made a lot of memories. When I went hiking, I followed in my father's footsteps by climbing the trails despite my small stature.

I would sometimes get motion sickness when I was in the car, but when my dad was by my side, I would calm down quickly. Once I calmed down, I looked out the window from the passenger seat and enjoyed the view. When my dad took pictures, I sat down like a model and stared at the camera, and the photos are alive and well in the album.

For all seasons we were glued. In the winter, he would burrow into the blankets and curl up comfortably as if he had built his own little kingdom. I used to travel to the warmth of the place for a long time, dreaming of it. On the other hand, in the summer, because of the heat, I would spread out on the floor and enjoy the coolness with my whole body. Lying on the floor with your belly pressed close to each other, 'Sewol, Newol'

She has always been at the center of our family. Even on the highway that is jammed with traffic during the holidays, or at a rest area. He then went to the islands off the south coast (Wando, Oedo, and Geojedo) to enjoy the nature there, and also went to Princess Magoksa Temple to enjoy the peaceful atmosphere of the temple. In fact, there was no place in the country that Aga hadn't been.

Every moment was precious. Feeling the changes of the four seasons together and making different memories for each season, it gave us great joy. They weren't pets, they were true family members and friends. Her bright and energetic energy always had a positive effect, and her lovely appearance was like a shining star in her daily life. We sincerely loved this hope for that.

(A walk of sweet and sour cotton candy)

1-3 It's sweet

Sweetness was the youngest child, showing off a different charm from sourness. While Hope was calm, cat-like, Lucky, was more energetic. With an unstoppable curiosity, she explored every nook and cranny inside and outside the house. The unusually charming sweetness gave us a new flavor. After we brought Lucky here, our house began to come alive again. And as the years passed, he grew older and filled the emptiness he felt after Hope left. She quickly became a part of our family.

There were many times when the sweet and sour cotton candy was finished. When Hope was still healthy, the two children spent a lot of time looking at each other. She took care of her like an older sister, and she learned from her sister's actions.

His appearance was markedly different from the first. Her tiny, button-like eyes seemed to contain the innocence of a child. The densely packed nose and mouth added to the loveliness. Lucky's face, which had a different charm from Hope's big eyes, was always bright and charming. The long legs were also one of the striking features. Every time she went for a walk, she was slender and walked briskly with her long legs, which was as elegant as a model.

Her fur was more like that of her birth mother, unlike Hope, who was semi-curly. And thanks to the subtle shimmering fur every time it was exposed to the light, it was shiny and gave off a luxurious impression. Another special feature was the pink jelly on the soles of the feet. Even when he became an adult, his pink color remained. The soft little jelly soles seemed to recreate the first's childhood. His appearance and personality were different from those of the sour ones, and he was loved by the whole family.

Thanks to the experience of raising the eldest child, Hope, it was easy for her to raise Lucky. From toys suitable for teething to grooming, to encounters with various puppies to develop social skills, to nutritious treats.

I learned that not all Maltese have the same personality. Cats usually hate water, but just as there are aquatic cats that can only be met after three generations of virtue, Lucky was so gentle with the Maltese.

She was as charming as her youngest daughter, and she was just a baby. Perhaps the influence of the mother, who had been domesticated by humans, was at work. At dinnertime, when the family gathered at the table, Lucky would invariably come up to him and turn him over and roll over as if to gently scratch his squishy belly. When I watched TV after eating, I would approach them one by one and flirt with them. When someone held out his hand, he rubbed his face in his hand to show his love. Aside from his fearsome gluttony, he was always on the verge of turning his stomach upside down.

Once Lucky had grown up to a certain extent, he began to shed his baby tee and show his personality. But the individuality sometimes clashed, especially in front of the rice bowl. The sweet and sour rice bowl wars were a common sight.

One evening, as dinner time approached, they heard the crackling sound of food being put into bowls, and the two cotton candy men ran to the kitchen excitedly. Hope hovered in place, wagging her tail, revealing her characteristic lively personality, while Lucky looked at her with a calm but piercing gaze.

As soon as the bowl of rice was placed on the floor, each one ran to his own bowl. But as he made his way to his bowl, he stuck his nose into it.

"Wang Wang!" he stomped. But Lucky didn't back down. Instead, he took a step closer and coveted Hope's vessel.

The two puppies faced each other and started a snowball fight. Hope barked and tried to protect her territory, and Lucky didn't back down despite her sister's warning that she was a little bigger. Instead, he took a step closer and coveted Hope's vessel.

In the end, both puppies stuck their heads into the other's bowl at the same time, not their own. Hope tilted his head as he sniffed Lucky's bowl, and Lucky looked satisfied as he explored Hope's bowl. At that moment, the two puppies began to eat from each other's bowls, as if they had made a promise.

"Mom, what if Luck and Hope fight again?" I asked cautiously.

Mom sighed and shook her head. "I'm really worried. It's a war to feed them."

Once again, as the two puppies rushed at each other's bowls at the same time, I grabbed Hope and Mom restrained Lucky.

"Lucky man, come here! I'll eat from your bowl!" she said softly, but Lucky still gave her a greedy look.

Hope looked at me with a frustrated expression. "I don't like food that much, but I'm lucky enough to eat it, so I think I'm jealous," I said, petting Hope.

Eventually, I took the two puppies to separate rooms and fed them separately. Hope ate from her own bowl, but she seemed to care about Lucky's room from time to time, and so did Lucky.

"Really, why do they covet each other's bowls so much?" she asked, shaking her head.

I replied with a smile. "Hope is jealous of Lucky, and Lucky is jealous of Lucky's food."

Mom nodded and soothed Hope. "Lucky man, your food is delicious. Now, let's eat comfortably."

Hope and Fortune were still coveting each other's bowls and barking at each other from the other side of the wall, often going into another room instead of eating. Just as people need to take away the ramen, coffee, and sweets that others have cooked for them, they will taste better. However, this armistice peace did not last long. When the chicken was delivered, it was a spectacle. When they finished paying with their cards and stepped into the living room with plastic bags, they started arguing with each other. In this case, I took care of the old and weak sour first.

"Hey guys, wait! Let's hope eat first~ Wait a minute for the youngest."

Lucky looked at me in frustration and barked aloud. "Wow! (Why is it that only my sister always comes first?)"

Stroking the youngest's head, he said, "Lucky, you're healthier. Hope is older now, and you need to take better care of him, okay?"

Hope seemed to understand what I was saying, and quietly approached the white flesh that had been peeled off. Lucky hesitated for a moment, but then stepped aside to settle down, as if he understood. "Yes, lucky. You just have to wait a bit. Soon you can eat too."

Hope took a bite and Luck handed a small piece to him. Good luck with this bite.

Lucky wagged his tail in delight. "Wow! (Thank you!)"

Hope looked at him affectionately and said. "Hope, eat slowly. Your health is the most important thing."

The youngest's cotton candy was meat, of course, and unlike the first, it was boiled egg yolk and broccoli. And after eating, he always played with his favorite brown stuffed dog by 'growling'. And the doll resembling the green Snoopy, who had been with him since he was a child, was used to sleep with his head cut off.

Lucky one's house was shaped like an Indian tripod. It was surrounded by a white cloth, giving it a cozy and warm feeling. When Christmas approached, the sticks in the house were wrapped in bead lights and decorated in the shape of a tree. It was cute and beautiful, like a little fairy house.

From an early age, he developed social skills, loved to socialize with other dogs, and was always at the center of their lives. However, due to a bad kneecap, he often limped, and his health was poor compared to the first. While Hope was strong in many ways, including her kneecap, internal organs, and skin ailments, Lucky had to be in the hospital frequently. I wondered where these differences came from, but a conversation with the vet solidified my suspicions into certainty.

When I go to the vet, I remember the conversation with the vet who examined Hope. "Hope is so strong, why does Luck keep getting sick?" and "The difference between a dog center and a home is clear. As luck would have it, commercially born puppies are often genetically unhealthy."

"Then what should I do?" I asked, and the vet nodded thoughtfully.

"If demand disappears in a capitalist market, it will never survive. Not buying a puppy from a dog center is the best solution. It's unfortunate that their livelihoods depend on it, but the first thing we need to think about is the welfare of the animals. If you really love animals, you need to stop doing things wrong."

I agreed. "It's the same with zoos. It's nothing more than a money-making scheme based on humanism. This baby is already part of our family and our relationship, but I think it will be even more important to find a dog at the abandoned dog center in the future."

The difference between hope and luck was not just a trick of fate, but the result of choice. I never regretted the choice I made to meet Uni. In the future, he hoped that many people's perceptions would improve and that the way they adopt would change. Sweet Cotton Candy was a puppy born into this reality. Although her body was weak, her heart was always warm and bright.

Just as I enjoyed cartoon movies on Tooniverse as a child, my dogs couldn't take their eyes off the television. In the scene where the animals appeared, he raised his voice and could not stand still for a moment. When I turned on the National Geographic channel, I saw fish swimming on the screen or lions or tigers hunting, barking and running in front of the TV. His ears fluttered and he crouched down in a prone position, pretending he was hunting, then raised his front legs and tapped the screen. When they played a show about animals, they were hooked.

THEY WERE TOGETHER throughout their civil service career. The sweet cotton candy I met for the first time in my adult life was always by my side even in my busy social life. One of my poignant memories is that when my family was out, if I didn't forget to close the door leading to the front door, I would wait for our family to come back on my scented shoes. The sight of his small body curled up on his shoes was both sad and adorable.

When I got home from work, I licked my nose and ran around the living room excitedly. Before I knew it, it was 12 o'clock at night. We went into the room together, and I said "good night" and put on a doggy classic. Lucky fell asleep soundly, relieved by the sound of the music, his heart pounding up and down with every breath he took. I woke up soon and went to my mother's side, but when I looked at the baby angel sleeping under the covers, I felt like all the fatigue of the day was gone.

Luck was both short and long. Even in the midst of my daily routine, the feelings I felt were sometimes filled with joy and sometimes with regret. Thanks to the pure love and affection of my youngest, I was able to become stronger and a better person in the midst of exhausting relationships. In this way, sweet and sour cotton candy has given us endless joy and happiness. It is now an irreplaceable memory.

(Hope is 15 years old / Luck is 3 years old)

EPISODE 2 COTTON CANDY which the sky ate

WHEN I WAS IN HIGH school, my dad and sister were talking on the couch in the living room. A gag concert was being rebroadcast on TV, and outside the window, a red sunset was embroidered in the sky before darkness fell. I was sitting at a table memorizing English words.

"Heesun, do you know the origin of the Maltese?" asked Dad.

"Well... I don't know, Dad. But I thought the Maltese resembled cotton candy," he replied with a laugh.

"Cotton candy?" asked Dad in surprise.

"Yes, Dad. Do you know how cotton candy is made?" she asked, looking at her dad with twinkling eyes.

"Well, I don't know about that, but you know what?" he asked.

"Yes! In the late 19th century, William Morrison and John C. Wharton used a machine in the United States to heat sugar and spin it into thread-like strips. That's the beginning of cotton candy!" he replied.

As I listened with interest to their conversations, I suddenly wondered if the origins of the Maltese and cotton candy were actually similar. So I went into my room and searched the internet.

"The Maltese originated in Malta about 2,800 years ago," he said, looking at the search results. "It was kept as a pet by the aristocracy of ancient Greece and Rome, and was considered special for its elegance and intelligence."

"Really? The Maltese has a long history," and "Like cotton candy, the Maltese has been loved by many."

Dad looked at us with a smile. "Heesun-ah, you were right. Both Maltese and cotton candy give people sweet memories and happiness."

I wrote down this story. Like the origins of the Maltese and cotton candy, we hope that our memories will remain as precious memories that will never melt.

The sour cotton candy 'Hope' that has always been with me since my school days

When I was in elementary school, I used to run around following the white smoke from the fart car. When I entered middle school, I played on scooters and rollerblades. And I was used to seeing my mom coming out behind me with a leash.

"Wow, you guys are so good at cornering!" said one of my friends.

"Would you like to try Hope?"

Hope wagged his tail and said, "Meng! Meng!"

"You really like to play with us, Hope," her friends said, petting her.

Mom ran around by Hope's collar, and we followed. And when I went to the pool, I could see the inside of the pool through the transparent glass of the rest room. Hope was there watching me swim.

"The pool water is so cool!" one of my friends yelled.

"That's right, swimming is best in the summer," I said.

Looking into the common room, cotton candy, which hates water to death, wagging its tail wildly across the walls. They seemed to be cheering us on by tapping them with their front paws.

"Look, Hope is watching us!" said his friend, waving his hand.

"Hope, wait a minute! We'll be right back," I exclaimed.

Hope nodded as if he understood.

A Fleeting Runaway: The Moment My Heart Sink

In the early 2000s, many neighborhoods left their doors open. My house was mostly closed, but that day I inadvertently opened the door and went to the grocery store. It had only been a little over ten minutes, but there was no hope in the house.

"No!" he said, and his heart sank.

It was an emergency. 'Where did Hope go?' she screamed, and hurried out the door. "Hope! Hope!"

Run down the stairs and shout, "Hope!" At the moment of shouting, I arrived on the 12th floor. There we found Hope sitting looking at our lake. The sour cotton candy sitting in front of the door waits for him, as if he knew he had gone out in the wrong way and had been waiting. When the elevator opens, it's right in the middle of the door on the left, which is exactly the lake of our house.

He looked at me and said, "Why are you here now?" I had a look on my face. I racked my head and was so grateful that my precious life was there.

I breathed a sigh of relief as I walked home with Hope. From that day on, I carefully checked the door to make sure that Luck and Hope didn't follow me when I went out. The moment when the cotton candy went somewhere and almost lost it still makes my heart ache.

Dad's commute to work and outings

When she was in high school, she woke up every morning to hear her dad wash her clothes, and she looked up slightly. Even as I dozed off on the bed, I knew my dad was going to work. At that time, he would just see him off at the door and then go back to his seat to sleep.

At the same time, I was whining from the time my dad washed up to go out. And as soon as I put on my shoes, I scratched my dad's thighs and said, "Take me with me!" I spun around as if to say.

Mom: "It's amazing how Hope can tell the difference between going to work and going out. It's the same way you wash up and come out, but when you go to work, you're quiet, and when you go out, you whine about taking me with you."

Dad: "That's what I mean. I'm curious too. Do they know the day of the week, do they know the subtle differences in my behavior, do they even recognize my feelings?"

Mother: "Well, I guess the way you walk is different when you go to work than when you go out."

Dad: "He's so clever. When I wake up at the same time every day and see how I'm getting ready, I can tell the difference."

Mom: "Thank you so much that we are the only ones who know each other."

Encounters in the Army

After completing his training as a soldier, he was assigned
to his own unit. And for the first time, I was able to visit him.
My maternal grandmother and grandfather also came, bringing
chicken, fruit, pig's feet, and Chinese food to the point where
the table broke. There was a variety of food on the table, and
the abundance made me realize my family's love for me.

My grandmother looked at me and said, "Oh, my
grandchild's face is half full. The training was very hard," my
grandfather said. "Still, I've become very confident. It was a lot
of hard work."

At that moment, Hope spotted me and rushed over with
rough steps. Watching that little body sprint toward me
touched my heart. He came in front of me and greeted me
with a wagging of his tail, and my eyes warmed up as I saw his
warmth.

As if all the longing and affection had poured out at once,
Hope rubbed her face against my legs and arms. Then he began
to gently lick my charred hands, as if comforting them. The
affection and longing felt on the warm tip of my tongue
enveloped me, and the fatigue of the hard training seemed to
be relieved a little. It was nice to meet my family, but it was
even more special to feel the pure love of cotton candy again.

After a brief first visit, he returned to military life. When
I was a corporal, I was on ammunition duty one day. In the
dark of dawn, when the cold winter wind was blowing like a
blade, I missed Hope so much. The ammunition depot was a
quiet, cold place. When he was bored at work, he sang Kim
Beom-so's "I Want to See You." "I miss you... That's all I can
say..." My singing echoed through the cold ammunition rack, as

if I wanted to reach Hope. Warm memories of the time with cotton candy came back to me, and my nostalgia grew even more. The sour cotton candy was the driving force that kept me going through every difficult moment. He was more than just a pet to me.

Memories at the Municipal Art Museum near home

The large lawn of the Municipal Museum of Art was a beautiful place with lush greenery and green lawns. The trees surrounding the lawn change color according to the different seasons, and the artworks installed here and there are in harmony with nature. On a sunny day, it was the perfect place to take a walk with the man-made fountain or spend time with the family.

We went to the Municipal Museum of Art with cotton candy. There was a couple sitting on a mat nearby, their baby. He is 3 years old, and he can't speak properly yet, but as soon as he saw the cotton candy, he ran to touch it. Hope ran across the lawn and hid behind a tree to wait for the baby.

When the baby walked around looking for hope, he quickly hid somewhere else. Taking advantage of the fact that the baby couldn't see himself behind his back, he continued to move behind another tree. While playing hide and seek, she seemed to know that she was making fun of the baby, so she sneaked out and aroused the baby's curiosity.

I was really surprised at this time. Is a dog intelligent this high? It was a game in which people recognized that they did not have eyes behind them. He also anticipated the direction the baby was looking for, quickly moved to the other side, and teased the baby. I didn't know they were so intelligent before I got a puppy, but it was at that moment that I understood that they were more intelligent than a human being 4 years old.

Reuniting with the Mother.

At the age of seven, her reunion with her mother took an unexpected turn. As a child, she may have had faint memories of breastfeeding and playing with her mother, but as the years passed, the image of her mother faded in her mind. One day, a mother dog with an aging appearance came to our house. I greeted the owner and the mother dog, but the daughter did not recognize the mother. Instead, they watched from afar, wary.

The mother dog likewise no longer remembered her daughter. At first, he approached slowly, then turned his head away, as if he had lost interest. I wonder how much time has passed, or maybe it's because we've changed so much in each other's appearances. Instead, she lowered her tail and tried to sniff carefully, but she couldn't hide her wary gaze. It was a little sad, but it also meant proof that cotton candy was now definitely a part of our family. The family reflected in the pupils of cotton candy was us. The soft voice of Daddy when he calls for Hope, the warm hand of Mom when he hugs her, and the laughter when she plays with me. All of this was a token of family for Hope.

Is hysterectomy really a good thing?

After the operation, he became rapidly senile. And he did not lie down, showing his belly. Perhaps there was some kind of trauma left behind. The ship was always full, full of vengeance. Even though I'm not a veterinarian, the question of whether it was right to force a knife into a healthy body ran through my mind. After the uterus was removed, she lay on her stomach, but she did not lie down and rest as she used to. Every time I walked, I took a rather heavy step. Maybe he still hasn't forgotten the memory of the operating table. The pain and fear of that day seemed to have left a deep wound in his heart.

I tossed and turned many nights. A sense of guilt weighed heavily on my heart that I might have made the wrong decision to force the surgery on my healthy body. Her abdomen was always swollen, unlike before the surgery, and she no longer regained her former vigorous shape. If I could go back to the day I decided to have the surgery, I wouldn't have had to deal with that pain if it was a female. It was a decision I made for the sake of her health and happiness, but I wondered if I had caused her more pain as a result.

Sour cotton candy that traveled all over the country

On a hot summer day, the memories are unforgettable at Haeundaejang.

"For love ~ let's travel. Let's go to the beach ~ Let's leave quickly! Yayayaya to the sea~"

On that day, it was crowded with tourists, and the sea breeze blew coolly. Cotton candy ran around the sand, full of curiosity about the sea she had never seen before. Every time his little paws touched the sand, tiny grains of sand bounced up and stuck to his white fur. When the waves rolled in, I thought about it for a long time, and then I dipped my feet in the water, and then I was surprised by the small waves and it was so cute to see them retreat. I laughed for a long time at the sight of such hope.

Hope was amazed to find small seashells and seaweed in every corner of the beach. Then, as he watched the waves roll in again, he cautiously approached the boundary where the water and sand meet. Sometimes, when the waves hit high, they would quickly step back, and it seemed to play hide and seek with the waves in a low voice.

Haeundae bought cold ice cream and sweet cotton candy among a variety of foods and shared them. Hope stared eagerly from the side, devouring the food that people eat. We took some cotton candy off, ate it in one gulp, and looked at us alternately.

"Haeundae is really nice on a summer day. The sea is beautiful, and the puppies look so happy," she said.

Dad added, "yes, it's nice to see Hope having so much fun."

When we were younger, we laughed and said, "Hope seems to love the sea just like we do. I'm so happy to be able to play with you."

In the afternoon, Haeundae Beach began to get even more crowded. After a blast on the sand, we rested under a parasol. As the cool sea breeze blew, Hope closed her eyes tiredly and took a nap.

As the sun went down, Haeundae was bathed in a beautiful twilight. The yellow-dyed sea and sand stretched out in a fascinating way, and the scenery of that moment was deeply enshrined in everyone's hearts.

The islands off the south coast (Wando, Oedo, Geojedo) and the trip to Magoksa Temple are also deeply engraved in my memories. On the boat to the island, I poked my head out in the wind and admired the surrounding scenery. Her big eyes were shining with so much curiosity. She ran freely in the beautiful nature of Oedo, and posed like a model when taking pictures with the blue sea of Geoje Island in the background. When I strolled around the tranquil temple of Magoksa Temple, I spent some quiet time enjoying the silence with the gentle breeze. In addition, they traveled all over Korea together. Each of these memories is collected and remains a precious treasure.

Sweet cotton candy with appointment and dismissal of civil servants

Every morning at 7:30 a.m., I get up, take a shower, and get dressed for a simple breakfast. At 8:15 a.m., I leave my house and head to the subway station. In crowded streets and crowded subways, it's just the beginning of a repetitive day.

The subway doors open and you leave. Amid a "rattle" sound, passengers from the next stop rush in. I stand in a familiar spot and hold the handle today.

"◇◇ ◇◇ ◇◇◇◇◇◇◇◇. ◇◇◇ ◇◇ ◇◇◇◇◇. The next station is Government Complex Station. The doors are on your left." ◇◇◇ ◇◇◇◇◇ ◇◇◇◇ ◇◇◇ ◇◇◇.

After moving from a large company to a civil servant, he pursued a stable life for seven years, but he grew tired of the boredom and repetitive routine he felt in the midst of it. Every morning at 8:40 a.m., I pondered deeply on the gray streets and crowded subway stations on my way to work. "Am I really fit to be a civil servant?, ha. Am I really the right person for my professional life?" I want to run for a higher dream. I want to do what I want to do!"

During the day, I worked on assigned tasks, wrote reports, and attended meetings. On the outside, her life was stable and regular, but inside she was in constant conflict. If you are looking for an answer to the question, 'Are you a civil servant?' I can say emphatically. Someone who can't do repetitive work in a conservative place that is stuck in a rut.

The six months before I left the company seemed like trudging through a tunnel with no end in sight. Every morning, I felt heavy as I left the house to go to work, and from the moment I opened the door to the office, I felt fatigue rush from the back of my mind. Even as I sit at my desk and get work done, the thought that keeps popping in my head is, 'What am I doing here?' It was a question.

In the monotonous routine and endless paperwork, I was getting tired of it. Everything seemed to fall apart, sleep didn't relieve fatigue, and every night when I lay in bed, I felt like I was losing the strength to face tomorrow.

Meanwhile, his relationship with his girlfriend, whom he had promised to marry, also broke down. As we exposed each other's wounds and exchanged accusations, we realized that our relationship could not be repaired. I sometimes think of my last conversation with her. After six months like that, I finally left the company. The moment I submitted my resignation, a heavy burden was lifted off my shoulders and I was afraid of the uncertain future.

The princess who started and ended with it was a sweet cotton candy. There have been countless gatherings over the course of seven years. Even if I came in late that day, there was a sense of silence in the quiet house at dawn with the warmth that greeted me. Lucky saw me smelling of alcohol and ran over to greet me without hesitation. The warmth that emanated from my body was the best remedy to wash away the fatigue of the day. After a quick wash, I passed by my mother, who was fast asleep. Then, as he patrolled to my bed, his footsteps were smooth and quiet. He climbed into bed and slept with me for a few hours, then went back to his mother's side, much like his adorable youngest child. If I hadn't raised a second child like this, I thought the Maltese were similar in personality, appearance, and intelligence, just like the first.

The sour cotton candy was generally very healthy, but had tear stains on the white hairs under the eyes, which turned red or brown, while the sweet cotton candy had few tear marks, despite the occasional recurrence of the skin disease along with the ear infection. As the youngest, she was very charming and endlessly sweet. And the difference greatly affected other personalities as well. Lucky liked things that were exceptionally pretty. He drank water from shiny crystal glasses rather than plastic ones, and he preferred pretty food bowls. Also, the dolls liked the princess-like dolls that the girls liked. He had a strong aesthetic desire, so he also focused on design when he wore clothes. And he was the naughty youngest.

Hope liked to eat kakka and meat, but Lucky also ate vegetables such as broccoli and cucumbers, and she was good at eating food.

There was also a big difference when I went for a walk. Hope walked on the sidewalk and explored her surroundings, but Lucky looked everywhere, grass, trees, and stones. I thought my gender had changed every time I walked around and marked without even trying. And he liked passers-by. I approached a group of people in the park and said hello. Whenever that happened, people would stop, touch the sweet cotton candy, and smile. "Oh my, that puppy is so cute! He's like a rabbit!" Every time the girls complimented him, he wagged his tail and was charming. The way he turned his head from side to side with his big eyes sparkling made it even more cute. When she heard compliments, she got even more excited, so she jumped up and down to people.

He had a gentle personality, but he was stubborn about his walking style. He insisted on his own specific route and liked to walk along the riverside. I quickly became friends with my walking mates I met in the grass along the stream. We spent pure time playing and smelling together. And on the day I went out for a walk with my eldest child, Hope, it was even more special. The sour cotton candy lovingly took care of the sweet cotton candy and obediently followed the sweet walking route. Sometimes, when the two of them walked side by side, the sweet and sour cotton candy was ready.

As winter approached, my sister sat on the couch in the living room and busied herself with needles. The red light from the electric stove warmly illuminated her hands, and the cotton candy stood beside them, staring sleepily at her brother. Thread by thread, strand was woven together, and finally a warm sweater was created. Hope's sweater was a soft pastel pink, and Lucky's sweater was yellow.

First, I put a sweater on Hope, and she obediently put it on. Hope wagged her tail as if she wanted to show off her new clothes.

"Now it's your turn of luck"

Mother: "You made it so beautiful. The two cotton candy are so cute."

Sister: "I don't have to worry about the cold weather."

On a winter day when white snow fell and a small pile of snow piled up on the roadside, the cotton candy enjoyed a walk at Princess Magoksa Temple. It was the day the whole world turned white. The finished sweet and sour cotton candy ran through the snow in tightly wrapped clothes. Then, along the snow-covered road, the tranquil scenery of the temple came in. Lucky seemed to see snow for the first time, and reacted to the strange white world with a white body. He ran around chasing the snow, trying to bite for a ball of snow. Curious to see the snow melt and disappear in his mouth, he tried it again and again, like a child. On the other hand, the familiar Hope left a small, light footprint every time she stepped on the snow, showing the force of a senior.

Mom laughed as she looked at the sweet cotton candy in her eyes and wondered. "It's my first time in snow, so I love it. I didn't expect you to be so excited," Mom said with a smile.

We waved to the two puppies and said, "Hope! Luck! Come here!" I exclaimed.

Magoksa Temple is a snow-capped mountain temple, and the white snow on the tiled roof adds to the serene beauty. In the silence, the sound of the dogs' footsteps and the laughter of the family members mingled. As they walked along the snow, the family felt the silence and serenity of the temple.

Dad said, "It's soothing to see the snow in such a serene temple."

After a walk like this, the long-awaited bath time comes.

Hope fidgeted back and forth every time she took a bath, hoping it would be over quickly. He seemed to be telling me to raise my front legs and take the bath as little as possible. Lucky, on the other hand, sat still, soaking in the hot water. The way they sat in the water looked like people enjoying a spa.

Hope and Luck both had their own personalities, but each time they taught, their personalities were on full display.

At first, I tried to tempt them with delicious snacks. "Sit down, Hope!" I commanded, and she looked at me and turned her head away as if to snort. I grabbed a more delicious snack in my hand and said, "Hope, sit down!" I ordered again. This time, he turned his head slightly, blinked, and pretended to dig on the spot.

"Hope, this is a delicious cracker!" I pleaded, waving my snack. Hope sniffed this time as if sighing. Then, as if to say, "You can't seduce me like this," he looked at the snack with a heaving.

He knew how to do it like sour cotton candy, but he only moved when he felt like it. The youngest, on the other hand, seems to have considered education a fun game. "Lucky you, sit down!" I immediately sat down. He flapped his ears, waiting for the next command. "Lucky man, get down!" he said, falling to the floor and looking at me with a wagging tail.

"Lucky, spin!" and "Lucky, high-five!" he said, raising his paws and tapping my palm and tilting his head at me. I decided to do something a little more challenging. "Lucky boy, dance!" I said, I can't do this. He scratched my thigh and said, 'Hurry up and give me a snack.'

I'm a flower-eating cotton candy

The veranda of our house was beautifully decorated like a small garden. Each of the 40 or so pots that my mother carefully cultivated had its own unique beauty. During the sunny day, bright flowers bloomed, and in the evening, the soft lights were lit up, creating a romantic atmosphere. Hope liked it and often plucked flowers and played, but Lucky didn't pay much attention to it.

One night, after dinner, my family was sitting in the living room watching TV. Hope and Fortune were at our leisurely side, when suddenly they heard a small noise coming from the veranda.

"What is it? Who's on the porch?" he wondered.

"Could it be that a worm as big as a moth has entered?" she guessed cautiously.

Mom smiled and said. "Hope and good luck go out onto the porch? You'll be able to figure it out."

I opened the door, and Hope stepped out onto the porch. Soon after, Lucky followed. Hope sniffed and examined every inch of the porch. As I walked through the pots, I gazed greedily at each flower that caught my eye. Suddenly, he spotted a small creature behind a large flower pot.

"Mon! Wall!" Hope barked softly.

Lucky was interested in hearing the sound, so he cautiously approached the back of the pot and found a small bird trembling with feathers puffing out.

"Oh my, Dad! There's a little bird here!"

Dad followed and took stock of the situation. "How did he get in? I think it came in through the window while flying. I've got an insect screen open here."

Mom said in a soft voice. "Well done, kids. Now let us help this little bird."

Dad and sister carefully put the bird in their hands and flew it out the window. From then on, when the sour cotton candy went out on the porch, she began to sneak and eat the flowers that her mother had grown, and the sweet cotton candy came into the living room in a flurry of sloppiness.

When it comes to the holidays, National Geographic is the best!

I visited my grandmother's house every holiday. The morning of New Year's Day was unusually busy. The whole family gathered, ate rice cake soup, and took turns. The two main characters, Cotton Candy Hope and Luck, also appeared wearing hanbok. Hope wore a red hanbok, and Luck wore a blue hanbok.

"Hope, luck, let's triple!" she said, and the two puppies tilted their heads. He looked puzzled, not knowing what it was, but when his mother showed him how to bow his head, he tried to imitate it. Hope stumbled a little away and sat down, while Lucky jumped around, wagging his tail excitedly.

"Our hopes and good fortune are tripled!" she beamed. "Now, take the money," she said, pulling an envelope out of her pocket and placing it in front of Hope and Fortune. Hope sniffed the envelope as she moved closer, and Lucky thought it was a toy and tried to bite it. "Oh, these guys! Don't bite that!" she said, taking the envelope in a hurry. "Be healthy and happy this year," Grandma added. Mom laughed when she saw it. "Grandma's rent money should go into your pocket, you bastards. That's how we get our snacks!"

"Grandma, thanks to our hope and good luck, I think you will be very happy this year!"

Grandma couldn't hold back her laughter and replied: "Yes, yes. Let's raise them well so that our family can all be healthy and happy."

And with a large grassy front yard, it was like heaven for the lucky ones. Running around the grass to their heart's content and enjoying their freedom was pure bliss. The front yard of my grandmother's house was a peaceful space where various flowers bloomed and trees cast shadows. Here I used to play with nature.

But there was another owner at my grandmother's house. It was my grandmother's cat. Lucky enough to get into a bout with the cat. The cat raised its paws on alert, and Lucky looked at the cat, wagging its tail. Their first meeting was tense. Every time the cat whispered, it ran away. Soon he was chasing after the cat again, and the cat climbed onto the high window sill and looked down at the cotton candy and frolic. Again, Hope didn't care if he thought he was a human being, and he hung limp on the heated living room floor.

Luckily, she used to be obsessed with the National Geographic Channel at her grandmother's house. The cat lost its curiosity and jumped onto the sofa in the living room. Then I played a National Geographic documentary. When the animal world footage showed a lion and a zebra racing for survival across the meadow, Cotton Candy stared at the screen for a long time.

His eyes were as small as buttons, and he followed the movements of the animals. As the lion slowly approached, and the zebra ran away, wary of its appearance, he stared nervously. It's like, 'Who are you?' He tilted his head as if to ask.

He stuck out his tongue when the birds flew into the sky, and when a big beast appeared, he stepped back slightly, but then got closer to the screen and focused on it, making him feel like the protagonist of a documentary.

I was lucky enough to spend every holiday at National Geographic. And when he got home from a trip or a holiday, he started running around the house in earnest and messing around the house. He would climb into bed and cry before going to bed, or go into the kitchen and rummage under the fridge and bark with joy when he finds a toy.

'After all, home is the best for dogs'

We have cotton candy with different flavors

Hope was always calm and like a grown puppy. And unlike outside, no matter who came to the house, he greeted them with a wagging tail. Lucky, on the other hand, was friendly to people she met outside the house, but she was wary of anyone who entered her home.

When I was in college, a high school friend came to visit me after a long absence. When her friend came home, Hope ran over and pretended to know.

"Hope really likes people," my friend said. "Why is Lucky so strange?"

I replied with a smile. "They're both Maltese, but their personalities are completely different, aren't they?"

The friend smiled and nodded. "I didn't expect the Maltese to be so different."

Lucky couldn't resist his mischievous curiosity, and it wasn't until he approached his friend and smelled it that he let his guard down a little. His friend held out his hand and stroked him, and then he began to flirt with his friend, wagging his tail gently.

Hope followed her dad best. Every time he came home from work, when he heard the sound of the front door being clicked, he would wag his tail and run to greet him. Moreover, on the day he returned home after a long absence, he jumped even more energetically, and the only sound in the living room was the sound of da-da-da-da.

Lucky, on the other hand, followed her mother best. Whenever Mom was in the kitchen cooking or doing chores, Lucky would hover next to her and get her attention. For a while, Lucky greeted his dad with a wagging of his tail when he got home from work, but then he went back to his mom and flirted with him.

In the evening, the two cotton candy went to their respective beds. Hope liked to sleep next to her father. When Dad sat on the couch reading a book or watching TV, he lay comfortably next to him, blinking sleepy eyes. And when Dad went to bed, Hope followed him and headed to dreamland beside him.

She loved to sleep next to her mother. I had already climbed on the bed and settled down. When her mother lay down on the bed, she would snuggle next to her and fall asleep feeling the warmth of her life. The two puppies slept peacefully with the other by their side.

That night, my friend smiled when she saw the cute behavior of the two dogs. "Your dogs have different personalities, different personalities, and they're really weird."

Sweet and sour cotton candy that's more powerful when clumped together

When I was a civil servant, I took a long annual leave, and Hope and Luck went on a special trip to Jeju Island with us. The boat from Yeosu to Jeju Island is a large and spacious ferry, and I booked a sweet pet room room where the dogs are VIPs. It can be taken out of the cage and has various amenities such as pads and beds for dogs.

Lucky seemed a little nervous about his first boat trip, but Hope was calm as a senior who had traveled all over the country.

"It's okay, Yun-ah. You're safe here," she said, petting her.

Dad nodded and said, "Yes, Ooni. I'm with hope, so don't worry, let's enjoy it." ", he added.

Hope snuck up to Luck and lightly touched his nose to comfort him. After resting in the guest room for a while, I wandered around the facility with my dogs. I was surprised that there was an escalator, and there was also a café, a rest room, and an observation deck, so I could spend time with cotton candy. In particular, the view of the sea from the observation deck was superb. Looking at the panoramic view of the sea, the family was full of anticipation for their trip to Jeju Island. The babies also enjoyed the cool breeze and looked at the sea happily.

"It's really cool! Hope, lucky, there will be more fun things to do when we go to Jeju Island," Mom said.

My sister also excitedly said, "That's right, what are you going to do on Jeju Island? Seeing the sea and eating delicious food. ," he added.

The boat sailed for about 6 hours, and we took our first step on Jeju Island, which is famous for its clean air and beautiful scenery.

We arrived in a rented car at a small guesthouse near Seongsan Ilchulbong Peak, a quiet village at the eastern end of Jeju Island. The elderly lady of the inn welcomed us warmly, and there was also a large yard for the dogs.

After unpacking, the family began preparing dinner at the barbecue at the back of the inn. My dad and I started grilling the meat on the barbecue grill, and my mom prepared fresh seafood and veggies. The two cotton candy jumped from place to place, dedicated to smelling new and clear.

As the sun went down and darkness fell, a large dog suddenly appeared in the distance. The dog was a stray dog that had been stray near the guest house, growling warily at strangers. Hope moved quickly and circled around the unfamiliar dog, attracting its attention, while Lucky stood firm and made a gesture of protection to Hope.

"Hope, lucky, be careful!" he said calmly, and I got up from my chair to pick up the two cotton candy pieces to safety.

At that moment, Hope circled around the strange dog with her quick footwork, and Luck began to follow her sister in circles. It could have led to a dangerous situation, so I approached fairly quickly and picked up the babies from the unfamiliar dog. And he seemed hungry, so he gave him meat and water.

When I thought about it when I gave the black stray dog water and meat, I was happy to see that the two little cotton candy were trying to cooperate, and that the two of them were relying on each other.

The next morning, I woke up early and headed to the Sunrise Peak of the Holy Mountain. The girls loved to go for walks, but this climb had a lot of steep hills and varied terrain, so I carried them up as much as I could. After letting go for a moment, Hope moved ahead, curious, and Lucky cautiously followed her.

"Go slow, Hope!" her mother told her to slow down, but she didn't stop. Then, suddenly, I lost my footing. For a moment, he lost his balance and almost slipped, but Lucky, who was right behind him, quickly swooped him off with his body and ran away.

"Well done, lucky!" he praised, but Mom was so surprised that she asked him to go back with the two cotton candy in his arms. Even then, I thought, are these guys coming to a remote place and trying to help each other? I thought again.

After descending the Sunrise Peak, we headed to the traditional market. It was crowded with a variety of food, specialties, and people. The cotton candy was sniffed everywhere in their cages, excited by the new smells and sounds of the market.

"This is the traditional market of Jeju Island," Dad said, guiding the two puppies around. "We're going to have a lot of snacks here that we're going to love."

Curiously, there was a stall on the side of the market with all kinds of dog treats. Dried sweet potatoes, chicken breast jerky, and organic dog treats specially made from Jeju Island caught my eye.

"Look, Hope and Luck are the perfect ones," Mom said. Hope and Fortune immediately walked over to it and sniffed it.

The stall owner laughed and said, "These sweet potatoes are dried in the traditional way. The dogs love it." He explained.

On the way out of the market, we decided to stop at a small café. There was a sign at the entrance of the café saying that dogs were allowed. The inside of the café was still crowded, like in the market, and there were other dogs on one table.

"Let's take a break here," Dad said.

At that moment, there was a loud noise in the corner of the café. The owner accidentally dropped the plate and broke it. People screamed in surprise, and the dogs started barking.

Hope sat nervously, her tail down, and Lucky sat next to her, as if to reassure her that Hope was clinging to her.

After a day at the traditional market, the family ended their trip with a walk along the beautiful beaches of Jeju Island. Hope and Luck jumped excitedly to the sand and the sound of the waves on the beach.

"It's time for us to go home."

Traveling on Jeju Island gave us memories like sweet and sour cotton candy for the first time.

A Day at the Dog Fair

In autumn, when the autumn leaves were dyed with colorful leaves, Hope and Luck took them to a large-scale dog fair in Seoul. This expo is an event that introduces a variety of activities and products that can be enjoyed with dogs, and is a place that dog lovers should visit.

Early in the morning, many people lined up with their dogs at the entrance. The fairgrounds were vast, with booths dotted with glittering products and colorful decorations.

"Wow, this is a dog fair! You're excited, aren't you?"

Hope and Fortune wagged their tails gently and looked around curiously.

As soon as I entered the fair, the first thing I saw was the booths selling dog supplies. A wide variety of toys, clothes, and treats caught my eye. Hope and Luck were also interested in the snack corner. We got a bunch of samples and had the two dogs taste them.

"This dried sweet potato treat looks so good, Hope loves it."

Next, we visited a dog grooming booth. Here, I was able to experience grooming services and bath products for dogs. Hope doesn't usually like hairdressing, but lucky has a love for water, so she decided to try it. And before I knew it, I was in a good mood, and I smiled broadly at us.

While walking around the fairgrounds, I found a dog playground booth. This is a space where dogs can run around freely, and various obstacles and playground equipment are installed. We released two cotton candy here. Each of them explored and played with the rides. Hope went through a small tunnel, and Luck ran on the high platform.

Then we headed to another highlight of the show, the photo booth. Here, I was able to take pictures with my dog in a variety of themed backgrounds. Hope dressed up as a cute rabbit, and Lucky dressed as a cool pirate. After taking pictures, we watched a dog training demonstration. A professional trainer showed the dogs a variety of training techniques, and Hope and Luck watched with interest.

In the car, Hope and Luck were tired and fell asleep on their cushions. I looked at the two cotton candy and stroked them lightly.

"You had a lot of fun today, didn't you? I've been happier with you guys."

The drug that the whole world allowed: oxytocin

As the two angels, cotton candy, lay on their backs, I quietly put my ear to the beat of my heart. Their beats and my heartbeat were at odds, but as time went on, they seemed to be more and more in sync with me. Every time I listened to their hearts pounding, I could feel the most precious life force in the world. And when I rub my face against the hair on my chest, I get a little bit of squirt, and finally, a black and pink jelly.

When you pet a dog, your body releases a hormone called oxytocin. This hormone is responsible for promoting bonding and affection. It evokes positive emotions in both dogs and humans, and is said to provide emotional stability and happiness. The connection with them brought solace in many aspects of my life.

Even though we weren't perfect, we were learning the value of life through each other's existence. These moments came together to form a strong bond with the princesses, and they finally found the meaning of their lives together.

2-1 At the edge of the rainbow bridge

By the time Hope was 15 years old, her body was getting older. He didn't run around as briskly as he used to, and even when he went out for a walk, he quickly got tired. His eyes are cloudy with a membrane in his eyes, which were once clear. Poop and pee were often spilled before going to the pad, and his body was slowly losing its shine. When he was taken to the hospital, he discovered a number of health problems that he could experience as an elderly dog. We prepared good food, gave them the medicine they needed, and gave them as much love and attention as possible. Even though she looked tired, Hope looked at me and wagged her tail. Every little gesture was lovely. We whispered in Cotton Candy's ear.

"She's always pretty, she's a beautiful princess. Let's be healthy baby"

Two years passed, and the 17-year-old grew more and more senile. One day, I came home late at night from a company dinner. My mom was going to a relative's funeral and texted me to come home quickly, but I wasn't in a position to do so. When I opened the front door, the house was quiet, and I didn't see any hope.

"Where's Hope?" I called cautiously. There was no sign of anything. Only luck kept me calm. As I looked around the house, I heard a faint sound coming from the veranda. As I approached, I saw Hope bouncing back and forth against a pillar in the corner of the porch, unable to get out.

"Hope, I'm sorry...I'm so sorry...I carefully picked her up and warmly embraced her. He had been outside for so long, so his body was cold, and his little chest was beating fast. I couldn't stop crying when I thought about how long that little creature had been in pain. I held her in my arms and whispered quietly. "Thank you so much, Hope. I'll never forget all the times we've been together. You know how lovely you are, don't you?"

Hope seemed to understand what I was saying, silently gasping for breath in my arms. He put the angel to bed and kept petting her, and he took a trip to dreamland. Lucky, who was watching the situation, wondered if she knew her sister's feelings or not, so she climbed the stairs and climbed the bed and hoped lay down next to her.

After that, Hope kept going to the corner. I would go into the corner of the bathroom, behind the sofa, into the dark, narrow space of the porch. As if preparing to say goodbye to the world, it was heartbreaking to see him lonely looking for a corner. Gone was his cat-like independence, and he was restless and whiny without his family. When he was able to walk even a little, he slammed his head against the wall and struggled to find us. And as he spent more time lying on his side, he swept his weak tail and shook the floor whenever he heard his family's footsteps. Lucky Yi, who watched Hope breathe heavily day by day, barked quietly with sad eyes. Still, I was grateful to heaven just to be able to feel the warmth of the first princess.

Suddenly, I thought, 'Am I a good protector for you?' I thought to myself. I've only now learned and understood a lot, but I wonder if I've been deceived by familiarity and neglected. I could have given you more love and care....

Before the sour cotton candy went to heaven, my dad had to leave home for a month to do business in Daegu. It seems that Hope waited for her father, who was the favorite in the family, even when her life was in danger. A month later, Dad came home.

Dad opened the door and called out to two angels, Hope and Luck.

"Hope, lucky! Daddy is here!"

The baby, who had been lying helplessly, slowly lifted her head. His legs trembled, his body shaking, and although he couldn't see or hear him, he felt him with his whole body.

Lucky excitedly circled around to greet him. Dad first gently picked her up and said, "Hope, I've missed you so much. Let's rest at home for a while and then go to Daegu." Lucky rubbed his face against his dad's arm and flirted with him.

The next day, Dad left for Daegu with two cotton candy. In the car, Hope sat on her mother's lap and looked out the window. Lucky sat in the back seat, wagging his tail excitedly and looking out the window. After arriving in Daegu, he took the two angels and entered an apartment near his business site. "Hope, let's stay here with Daddy for a while," Dad said, carefully putting her down and walking around the house with Lucky, helping her adjust to her new surroundings. The next day, however, the sour cotton candy had to leave at 2 p.m.

We were coping with our grief by keeping the memories with our eldest princess and making new memories with our youngest. Sweetness gave love in a different way than sourness, and as a member of the family, it wiped away our tears.

After six months, I gradually returned to my daily routine and focused on the repetitive work life and marrying my girlfriend.

Around the time I decided to leave the company, I remember my last conversation with my girlfriend, who worked for a public company. That evening, we sat down at our usual café. She sighed, holding her coffee cup in her hand.

"He's been having a hard time lately," she said. "Is it because of work at work?"

I nodded. "yes, I'm so tired. It all feels pointless. I don't have a goal in life. I'm thinking about quitting."

Her face hardened. "So what do we do? Just quitting a stable job?. Is it the right choice for our future?"

"I know," I replied. "But I don't think we'll have a future if I'm so tired. You know that. Our relationship has been going through a lot lately."

"If you feel that way, I don't know what to do. No matter what I do, I'm tired of the conversations that are repeated every day. And I don't think it's getting any better."

I took her hand. "I'm sorry for you. I'm so sorry. I can't make you happy.", "I can't keep going on like this. We... Let's stop here."

My heart was broken, but she was right. They were very tired of each other.

"Yes, you're right. Let's end it here."

From that day on, we went our separate ways. After she left, it hurt me all the more to be alone, but at the same time, I felt that it was the right decision for the two of us.

On the one hand, I said goodbye, but I still wanted him to get through it with me and stay by my side. The conversation that day was so duplicitous and paradoxical in its complexity.

After leaving the company, I went out with my youngest at 7 a.m. However, the lucky princess, who loved to go for a walk, suddenly stopped walking and gave me a look to hug her. I thought something was wrong, so I went to the vet I used to go to often. The first name I heard there was anemia. When Lucky's health suddenly deteriorated, anxiety began to creep up on her. Before the pain of parting with the eldest princess had subsided, the youngest child's staggering body was filled with immense pain. At such a young age, I never thought there would be a red flag for my health...After going to the hospital, I ran around the house and thought I had found my health. I thought it was a temporary anemia that women suffer.

On another day, the sun was high and cloudless. The cicadas were already chirping. Leaving the apartment complex, we began to walk towards the perimeter path. The asphalt road wasn't hot yet, but it was enough to make me feel like summer was just around the corner.

Lucky seemed to be out of energy today. Normally, he would have run around cheerfully, but his steps were heavy. I felt something was wrong, but I thought, "Maybe it's not a big deal," as I walked on the sidewalk. Suddenly, the baby stopped. His breathing quickened, his body slumped backwards, and he collapsed with a glance.

For a moment I was so surprised, "Lucky!" But all he could see was his narrowed eyes. I didn't know what to do, so my heart raced and my head went white. I couldn't believe what was happening in front of me.

When he saw him lying helplessly on the floor, he didn't have time to hesitate. I picked her up carefully and started running to the local small veterinary clinic. The asphalt road was still warm, but my heart was freezing.

"Please, I hope everything is fine...I prayed to myself.

As soon as I arrived at the vet, I urgently explained the situation to the vet. "My dog suddenly collapsed. The vet quickly took him away for a checkup. I just stood by and waited anxiously. During the consultation, the veterinarian, who had been in charge of my health since I was a child, said with a serious expression:

"Lucky right now, this condition is difficult to treat in our hospital. I think you need to go to a big hospital right away. Get a closer look there."

I called my mom to inform her of the situation, and headed to a big hospital first. When I arrived at the hospital, it was vast and overflowing with high-tech medical equipment. The white wall tiles stood out, and as I walked through many rooms, I saw the hospitalized puppies. Veterinarians and nurses were busy, taking care of the animals.

After completing the procedure at the counter, we went upstairs and was greeted by a veterinarian in his early 30s at the entrance with a gentle expression.

"Lucky guardians, aren't you? Come this way."

I went into the examination room. The vet said that after taking a closer look at the condition, Luck needed blood tests and x-rays. A few minutes later, he looked at the report and began to explain with a serious expression, like a veterinarian at a small veterinary clinic.

"Lucky to be out of red blood cells right now. His condition is quite bad and requires an immediate blood transfusion. If you don't have a blood transfusion, it can be dangerous."

We were all shocked to hear this. Mom spoke first.

"Can I get a blood transfusion right away?"

The vet nodded. "Yes, blood transfusions are available right away."

Without hesitation, we went straight to the hospital, and Lucky lay in the hospital bed ready to go. When the needle was inserted into the vein to receive a blood transfusion, I could not hold back my tears as I saw my body trembling. Seeing Lucky Man breathing heavily, he prayed fervently in his heart.

"Please, you must get better, you can do it, lucky one."

'Love, strangely enough, is that the one who loves more, the more must endure. I want to love you more, so that I can be sick and in pain.'

"But, no matter how much I think about it, I feel that your love is greater than mine."

The vet continued to explain Lucky's condition and treatment plan to us, and the nurses checked on him. In the meantime, I was having a hard time fighting my illness with my small body. All we could do was watch from the sidelines and cheer them on. In this way, Lucky was able to fight his illness, and we often visited the hospital to check on his condition, and we had a hard time together.

After the first discharge from the hospital, Lucky became more and more unable to use himself as his condition worsened. When his little body couldn't resist gravity and collapsed, he somehow made the princess feel comfortable. As her health deteriorated, she felt that her time with her was running out. After going through the separation from Hope, my heart was heavy at the thought of having to endure the grief and pain that came again. But I wanted to make sure that she was loved until the very end. Every night I slept next to him, praying that I could sleep as comfortably as possible.

(1st blood transfusion)

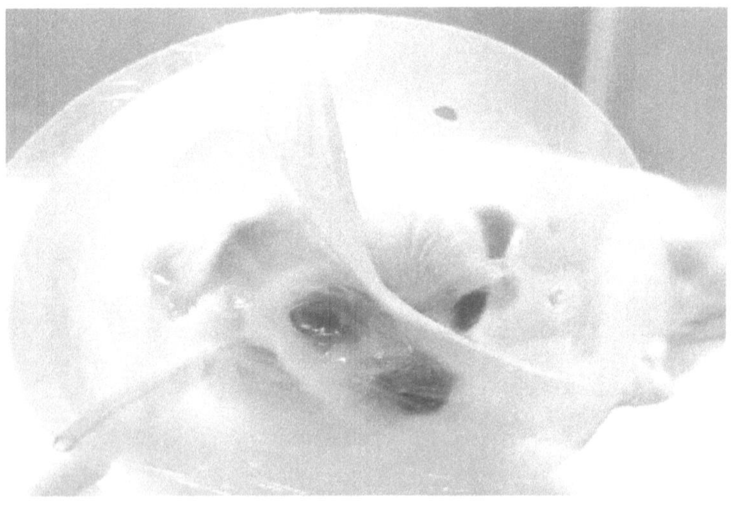

(2nd blood transfusion)

2-2 Please come back

Sour cotton candy

Hope, who had gone to Daegu, had been healthy and energetic until yesterday, but quietly left us. When my parents came back from a 30-minute absence, what they saw was so sad and heartbreaking.

When Dad and Mom got home, they found Hope in the corner of the kitchen, where they were getting cold. Dad approached her and spoke to her, touching her stiffening body with trembling hands.

"Hope...Daddy is here. I'm sorry, this happened while I was away for a while..." Dad's voice trembled, and his eyes filled with tears. Her mother sobbed next to her and patted her on the head.

"Hope, you're here. Didn't our hopes hurt a lot? Don't get sick anymore and rest in peace...."

My mother burst into tears at the end of every sentence and couldn't speak properly. Embracing Hope's cold body, the two of them couldn't stop crying for a long time. Dad caressed Hope's little face and continued.

"Hope, you've been through a lot. Every moment of your life has been a great joy for us. Thank you, thank you so much...."

Mom whispered to her tear-stained face as she pressed her closer to Hope.

"Our hope, you were such a nice, good boy. Now you can run around in heaven to your heart's content. My mom loves me a lot...."

Eventually, the angel's body could no longer hold on and quietly left us. On the day I left for the dog, I was on the phone with my parents and overwhelmed with grief beyond words. Is it a joke of the gods? He didn't know if it was fate.

Mother: "I wish you had been...Hope looked so energetic that day. The child, who had been weak the day before, was running around as if he had recovered his health."

Dad: "yes, how well you eat. I was just like I was when I was 5 years old. After eating without any leftovers, he seemed to have fully recovered."

Me: "That's why you took the video. We were relieved to see that...I didn't expect to leave like this."

Brother: "Hope was going to show us one last time that she was going to show us her liveliness."

Mother: "There are times when the day before you die, your soul is clear, your mind is sober, and you act like a normal person. Or maybe Heesun wanted to show her one last healthy side, as she said."

Dad: "I think I wanted to have one last happy moment before Hope left us. I can still see how happy he looked that day."

Me: "I think Hope endured the pain at home at the end of her life and waited for her father to come. And when I saw my dad, I left."

Brother: "It hurts me to think of Hope that day, but it's also comforting to know that I was happy at the same time."

Mom: "Hope has given our family so much love and happiness. I think he thought of us until the last moment. I'll never forget what it looked like."

Dad: "Okay, let's all cherish the time we had with Hope. I will continue to live with that love in mind."

After Hope's departure, his soul went to heaven, but his flesh remained in our sorrows. Looking at the white body that had returned home from Daegu, the reality that he had really left this world touched my heart deeply. His body was limp, and his small frame felt even smaller. Even as I looked at the lifeless body, I looked at the closed eyes, tears streaming down my eyes, as if they would open their eyes again and look at me.

Lucky kept asking to see if she knew her sister had gone to heaven or not. When he showed her a glimpse of her body on the cushion, Lucky slowly approached, sniffed it, and touched her with her paws. She kept hovering around her, as if she was trying to wake her up. I checked my sister's body several times with that little nose, and for some reason it seemed to be staring at me with tear-filled eyes.

The fur was still soft, but the warmth was gone. Lucky whined, then curled up next to her sister in exhaustion. As if she didn't want to let her go, she stayed by her side until the end. The joy of bringing Hope back for the first time and the many moments we had spent together flashed by like a flashlight.

The weather that day was a reflection of our feelings. For Hope's funeral, a nearby crematorium was booked for the weekend, and her favorite kaka, her clothes, and Tug toys were placed on the funeral shelf. The shroud was dressed in a light blue and pink hanbok. The whole family gathered to mourn for the baby who was leaving for the last time.

After the ceremony, we headed to the crematorium. No one spoke, but a lot of thoughts went back and forth. When we arrived at the crematorium, we said our last goodbyes to hope.

"I loved you so much, but to let go like this..." Mom said, wiping away tears.

"Hope has given us a lot of happiness. I'll remember it forever," Dad said calmly.

"That's right. The time I spent with Hope was so precious. The love she gave us will never end," she added with tears in her eyes.

After the cremation, I was given a sealed white porcelain ossuary. Holding a small ossuary in hand, the whole family gathered in front of it and recalled the moments they had spent with Hope.

The sour cotton candy will now rest peacefully in heaven. We took the ossuary home and placed it on a shelf leading to the main room of the house. Candles were lit and prayers were offered.

"Hope, you will never forget the time you spent with us. I feel like your warmth and love are still with us. I hope you can feel our love in heaven."

When I finished praying and looked up, I saw my youngest child, who had been quietly lying next to me. It was so lovely and pathetic to see her silently bowing her head in front of her ossuary, as if praying with her. Her white body looked even warmer in the soft candlelight. Her eyes were filled with longing for her, and my heart sank as I looked at her.

Lucky hovered by the ossuary for a while, wondering if he missed Hope. One day, he sniffed near the ossuary, as if trying to smell it. Then, before I knew it, I quietly fell to my side and fell asleep peacefully. As he stroked the youngest, he felt the warmth of his body and it seemed like they were all still together.

Parting with sour cotton candy was so difficult. It was hard for me to accept that the girl who had always been there for me was no longer with me. For the time being, sweetness filled the void of sourness and made new memories, but in order not to forget the time we spent with Hope, she cherished the photos she had taken together, the promenade with small footprints, and the things she had been.

Breakups aren't always easy. There are complex emotions inside. And in the process, they learn courage and maturity.

It's back to my daily routine. Repeated commutes, and love affairs.

The life of a civil servant didn't suit me too much, and I was so excited about the vacancy of Hope that I went on a trip to Haeundae before breaking up with my girlfriend. The night sea swayed in the darkness beneath the street lamps on the sandy beach. It was then that "as if shot" sounded ashore. "Like I've been shot~ My chest hurts so much~ In my punctured chest~" Each verse of the lyrics seemed to represent my heart.

Hope's absence felt too great. The repetition of going to work and leaving work, and even in love, there was a void. Every time I thought of the time I spent with Hope, my heart sank. Even in this moment with my girlfriend, I could hear the sound of the waves of Haeundae and the cry of Hope overlapping in my head.

It was a family trip, and in the midst of a large crowd, I vividly remembered the image of my baby jumping to avoid the waves every time they soaked my white feet. The surprised face every time that little foot got wet, and the moments when he ran around laughing again. Now it remains only as a nostalgic memory. We walked in without saying a word. My girlfriend quietly squeezed my hand. As her song continued to play, and even after the song ended, the longing in my heart soaked my heart like a wave.

Sweet Cotton Candy

Finally, he ended his seven-year career as a civil servant. And when I started the academy business, I had no idea that my second child, who was so young, was heading to the rainbow bridge. Lucky was hospitalized with a diagnosis of erythrocytopenia. Even in my busy life, every time I visited the hospital, my heart ached.

As soon as she entered the hospital, she found herself lying helplessly in the narrow walls of her room, with a large funnel around her neck. He had been in that cage for so long, and his eyes were full of frustration and anxiety. But as soon as they made eye contact with us, despite their pain, Lucky recognized us and immediately stood up and scratched the transparent wall with a whin. On the one hand, it was welcome, but at the same time, it was sad.

Every time the youngest princess moved, she could hear the funnel crashing against the wall. When the hospital opened the door, she hugged us, licking our hands and welcoming us. Tears welled up in her eyes, and she was so sad to see her wagging tail in response.

"Lucky man, you'll be fine. Let's try a little harder," but our hearts became heavy as we watched him. He cried and whined more, his voice as if he was begging him to go home, and it broke his heart.

Now that I think about it, the more time she spends in the hospital room, the more I realize how hard it was for her. I sat down with the vet. The examination room was quiet, and the expression of the teacher in the white gown was calm.

"The numbers are a little below normal, but I think it's best to go home and see what happens."

"Yes, I'm sure he's been in the hospital for so long, it's frustrating. I think it's best to take him home."

"I received two blood transfusions, but I didn't get better. If you have a second infection, please contact us as it is an emergency."

"Yes, sir."

As she was going through the discharge process, the green trees swayed slightly in the wind through the transparent windows of the hospital, and the child in her arms looked eagerly at them.

We walked 10 minutes in the summer sun. In the shade of the trees, I was able to escape the heat of the day, but the heat was still hot and beads of sweat beaded on my forehead. On the way home with my youngest child in my arms, the thin pink skin behind the child's fur was heated by the heat.

She had to receive a second blood transfusion immediately after the first blood transfusion, and she was worried about her health. Luckily, though, I'd been in a narrow, transparent walled space for so long, and even though it was a hot day, I sniffed and breathed in to fully soak up the breeze and sunshine.

As soon as I got home, I walked around the house picking up my cushion and around the house to see if I had any energy. And that day, I headed to dreamland peacefully. The next day, with a longing look in our eyes, we put our youngest angel in the stroller we had prepared in advance. At the tender age of seven, she could no longer walk on her own, so while she was in the hospital, she had to get a dog stroller. I put my baby in a cute little stroller and walked slowly along the path around the apartment. Lucky in the stroller looked around curiously.

The sun-drenched flowers along the roadside and the leaves of the trees fluttering in the wind caught his eye. Unlike the time he spent in the hospital, he was now free to enjoy the outside world, and he smiled. Sometimes, when I got out of the stroller and sat down on the lawn, even though it made my walk uncomfortable, that small gesture regained my vitality. Watching him do that, he held out hope that his youngest child would be able to recover.

In the arboretum, I pushed a stroller and strolled slowly in the shade of a tree. Lucky was still smiling brightly as he liked the sound of the birds and the wind whispering through the leaves.

For two weeks, we had a free time with Luck and a breath of fresh air. However, Lucky's condition was getting worse and worse again. His movements slowed and he lost his appetite. Even when I tried to feed him the food he liked, he wouldn't open his mouth. The days without water and crackers became more frequent.

The baby angel's body grew thinner and thinner, and she had to go to the hospital again. Eventually, a third blood transfusion was given, but it had little effect. On the contrary, a secondary infection occurred after the blood transfusion, which was life-threatening. As I walked through the corridors of the hospital, I heard the cries of Lucky in the hospital room. It was a whining, pathetic cry. It was as if they were screaming for help.

"Whine whining.."

Inside the room, Lucky moaned, breathing heavily. As the nurse gave her fluids with a syringe, she crossed her legs and cried.

"◇~~◇◇..."

The screaming cry tore through my chest. I wanted to keep it from hurting, but I didn't know what to do.

The hospital bills were also not negligible. One or two hundred blood transfusions at a time were the norm. But what angered me more than that was the wrong diagnosis and prescription. My sister is a doctor at Seoul National University Hospital, so when I checked the data at the time, I found out that the name of Lucky's illness was misdiagnosed. He was given a blood transfusion because it was a blood disease, but it caused a secondary infection and took his life. I felt that the veterinarian's negligence was obvious, so I had to consider a civil lawsuit.

I felt like I didn't know the world. I hated people even more because I thought it was all the fault of humans. I'm human, too, but I couldn't help but clench my fists.

Grief never came. On the day she returned home after her third blood transfusion, exactly four hours later, at midnight, she began to cry out and unable to control herself. As he walked back and forth, he slammed his belly on the floor, and a red liquid spilled out of all the holes.

Blood pooled on the floor. Dark red blood continued to flow from his mouth, nose, and even his anus. I urgently called the vet, but my condition was already too difficult to improve. I asked her to drink water, but she refused. Putting water in his nose didn't help. My heart sank at the sight of the baby crawling under the dark curtains and onto the porch floor.

In the end, Lucky laid him on a soft cushion. When the lights were turned off, all I could hear was heavy breathing in the dark room. As she groaned and writhed, I gently squeezed her hand. My whole body twisted and convulsed, and tears flowed down my face. Hoping she wouldn't feel any more pain, she had to watch Lucky's last. She rolled her eyes helplessly and looked back and forth between her mother and me. And he was staring us in the eye all the way, even though he was in pain.

"It's okay, it's okay. Get a good rest, baby."

Carefully stroking his forehead and head, he said: Lucky nodded slowly. It was as if he understood what she was saying.

Immediately, she fell into her mother's arms and quietly closed her eyes.

His head drooped helplessly under the force of gravity, and he couldn't hear his heartbeat. Then his whole body grew cold and slowly hardened. Still, he looked calm, not in any more pain. The youngest left us at 1 a.m. I could still hear his heavy breathing. I wanted to cry, but I couldn't get my voice out. There was only sobbing in the silence. The mother also shed tears and held the baby's hand, which was still warm. And finally, I washed away the sweet cotton candy with tears, runny nose and hot water.

The youngest angel gave us so much love. I can't forget the way she made eye contact with us, even though she was treated hard at the hospital. There was love in his eyes for his family.

The spirit departed, but I laid him down on a comfortable cushion to rest a little longer at home before going to the crematorium. And for three days, I kept telling him I loved him. The next morning, the wind blew in the middle of the season, transitioning from summer to autumn. In my dad's car, I stroked her head as I looked at her white fur, pink belly, and jelly on the soles of her feet. Outside the window, I could see the autumn leaves dying. The contrasting colors were so sad.

We headed to a crematorium nearby. For the funeral, she prepared her favorite kaka and the clothes she usually wore. And finally, Dad whispered as he touched the stiff body of Lucky Yi, who was wearing a fine white hanbok as a shroud.

"Rest in peace now, my youngest daughter. You've worked too hard."

Dad's voice trembled.

When I arrived at the crematorium, my mother continued to sob, and my sister had red eyes. We stood around the coffin of the lucky one and said goodbye.

"Rest in peace, my princess."

Her voice trembled. One by one, we said our last goodbyes to the coffin. And the coffin slowly entered the crematorium. The flames flared up, and the baby's body vanished.

Standing at the crematorium, I was sad to find this place again. It was only two years ago that I had to send my first princess of 17 years. This time, after my good fortune, I hated the world even more. I was so upset that I had lost my family because of the doctor's negligence. After the cremation of Lucky was over, I picked up the porcelain ossuary and headed home. The sun shone warmly into the car, and the white scent wafted through the tip of my nose. I felt the spirit of Fortune whispering to me with a smell.

A mixture of anger, resentment, and sadness made me feel that the world was unfair. There was no such thing as fate, it was just people's mistakes and incompetence that created the tragedy.

We huddled together in the living room. Dad let out a heavy sigh and said.

"Let's stop now. I don't want Luck to suffer."

Mom nodded, wiping away tears. "That's right. It's not right to drag this out for Hope's sake."

I held back my tears and said quietly. "But it's clear that the vet was at fault. If you go over like this, other pets will be harmed."

Dad looked at me quietly and said, "I fully understand our feelings, but let's not be vindictive. I don't want to hurt the youngest princess anymore."

My brother quietly agreed. "Yes, I know it's hard for us, but I don't want to hurt your precious memories."

In that moment, I decided to accept my family's decision. Remembering my youngest's bright smile and love, I looked at the picture of my youngest that night and said quietly: "I'll be stronger for you. I won't forget your love."

Looking at the traces of her youngest child left all over the house, she was overwhelmed with nostalgia. Now I enter the living room, and on the way to the master bedroom, there are framed pictures of the children's memories and candles with their favorite scents. Inside the frame are photographs taken with the two angels. Next to it were two small ossuaries.

I sat in front of the ossuary and played classical music. Lucky's favorite canon variations rang out. "Tudung Tu

The cheerful rhythm of the piano filled the space. "Ding Ding Ding"

The soft melody of the strings followed. He folded his hands and bowed his head. Tears welled up in my eyes. He hoped that Lucky's spirit would soar high into the sky.

A faint scent from the ossuary wafted through the tip of his nose. The scent was tinged with its own squirt and precious memories together.

"It's a mixture of babies. It's like we're here."

Mom told Dad. His eyes were red, but there was a small smile on his lips.

"That's right. The fragrance envelops this house on behalf of the lucky one's soul. And the scent of the babies reflects the happy times of our family."

My sister nodded and said, He looked at the frame and smiled wryly.

For a while, the fragrant fragrance of babies that filled the living room captured our senses. Just as it reflects the coexistence of good and evil, joy and sorrow, the fragrance was also enough to stimulate a wide range of emotions. The two princesses were a big part of my life, and the love and happiness they gave me was indescribable, so I had to cherish that time. Lucky filled Hope's void all along, but also warmed her heart with her special pranks and adorable deeds. It came in a different way than the sour cotton candy and gave it a sweetness in a different shape and form.

Remembering the cotton candy, I sat by the window. As I gazed at the sky with a rainbow, I was immersed in memories again. The fragrant smell of the hair on her chest still lingered on the tip of her nose. The fragrant squirts were the happiness of my nose, and the unfolded rainbow was the happiness of my eyes to indicate their presence.

'I'm going to be happy to be running around on clouds as soft as cotton candy.'

The smell of the squirt is my olfactory memory, the rainbow is my visual memory, and the sweet and sour taste of cotton candy is my taste memory. Never, cotton candy doesn't melt. The fragrance and love they left behind will remain forever in my heart.

(In winter, the skewers who liked the blankets on the hot sheets)

EPISODE 3 STICKY COTTON candy

Our family had a hard time after the babies left, but gradually we got back to normal.

I got into the academy business and the carbon credit relay business, and although I had one failure along the way, I didn't give up and kept moving forward. And when I have free time, I write about the princesses. The photos and videos of them bring tears to my eyes, but the beautiful memories they left behind are also very encouraging.

What kind of place is the puppy star where their souls dwell? And where could it be?

There is a planet floating high in the sky, or even in space, and that is the dog star. The bluish glow of the planet is kept warm. There are plenty of different playgrounds and places to play hide and seek. In the rainbow-colored forests, endless flower gardens, and small rivers flowing through it, dogs run free, splash around, and smell the fragrance of various flowers.

The ground of the dog star is soft and elastic, and it is ideal for running. The trees here are designed to be safe for dogs to climb, and there are sweet fruits that can be chewed, plucked, tasted and enjoyed at any time. The lake there is clean and clear, and it keeps a warm temperature for the dogs to swim in.

The sky is even more beautiful at night. Countless stars dot the sky, and the Milky Way is clearly visible. The Milky Way wraps dogs around them like a cozy blanket when they feel like resting. There are also guardian angel dogs with special abilities. These angels are responsible for their well-being and are always there to protect them. When puppies are playing, they are always on the lookout for any injuries they need, and they are given everything they need.

This planet has made it possible for puppies to repeat their happiest moments indefinitely. There is plenty of food and water, so you never go hungry or thirsty.

Time is meaningless in the dog's star. Time seems to stand still, allowing us to be faithful to the present moment. Puppies have the energy to run around endlessly. Suddenly, the classical music that the babies loved reverberates incessantly. Mozart's piano concerto and Beethoven's symphony form the melody, and the dogs run around excitedly to the melody. Maybe the babies are running around with them?

If you go down a little further in space and look closer, you will see that the rice bowl is full of kaka, which the cotton candy loved. Maybe the puppies that arrived on the planet ahead of time are taking care of the princesses' souls.

"Lucky you. It's too bad you left so soon, but at least you can be happy there, right?"

The first princess was also unfamiliar and awkward at first, but now she is happy to be friends with the dogs. The light and heavy howl of the first princess as she roamed the planet reached my ears.

I took a serious step into the puppy star. There was a familiar sound. It was the sound of the youngest's footsteps.

"Lucky!" he said, and he came running from nowhere. My youngest dog, whom I had missed so much, greeted me with a big smile and a tongue sticking out.

"How are you? How are you doing here?" I asked, and Lucky circled around, wagging his tail. Soon I licked my face. "I'm making a lot of new friends here and listening to my favorite classical music."

"Oh, do you know how to speak here? It's a big deal, isn't it?"

"Lucky you, there's Hope running around there. You look so happy."

Hope was still independent, but she fit in harmoniously with everyone there. They ran around and fro, playing among the wildflowers.

Luck was also a little away from me, wagging its tail and running around. They chased small butterflies in a field of cute flowers and played in the water by a babbling stream. With each splash, the cotton candy's face didn't melt. Hope is smiling brightly as she looks at Lucky Yi as if she has been waiting. And when Luck arrived at the Puppy Star, Hope followed as before. The two cotton candy who had not met in a long time ran around on the wide meadow to their heart's content.

"Lucky, are you going to set the course today?" she asked, barking briefly.

"That's right, sister. I'm going to take a more interesting route this time!" he replied confidently.

When he reached the entrance to the park, he swerved and jumped onto the grass. He hesitated for a moment, but then began to run on the lawn.

"What does it smell like here?" he said excitedly.

"Let's see...Um, it smells like a rabbit?" Hope replied, sniffing.

Lucky was so curious that he changed his steps again and ran to a small pond. He slipped and fell into the mud near the pond.

"Oh my gosh, lucky!" she said, unable to hold back her laughter. "You're so muddy!"

"Haha, that's part of the adventure!" he replied casually, brushing the mud off his body.

Walking side by side along the promenade, the two cotton candy stopped under a large tree. They circled around the tree and smelled new scents. There was a special secret. At the center of the Puppy Star was the Tree of Remembrance, which held the moments when the puppies were loved on Earth.

"This tree is so big and wonderful! The smell reminds me of my mom, my dad, my brother, and my sister!" said Lucky, admiringly.

"Yes, I come here often and remember them. Shall we rest here for a while?" she sat down in the shade of a tree.

At that moment, a small squirrel quickly descended from the tree. Lucky saw the squirrel and said with a twinkle in his eye, "Hey, why are you in the dog star? Let's play together!"

"I had a lot of fun today, lucky," Hope said to Lucky, who was stuck in a fleeing squirrel.

"I had fun, sister. Let's have a fun walk like this tomorrow!" he replied, wagging his tail excitedly from side to side.

As I touched the tree, I was reminded of the memories I had with the two cotton candy. The moments of the walks, the playtimes we spent together, and every little gesture went through my mind.

"You are happy here, hopeful, lucky," I said, tears streaming down my face. They looked at me, quietly approached me, rubbing their faces on my hands and face.

My sister had just arrived. As soon as she saw Hope and Luck, she began to cry. Soon, Lucky reached out to soothe her, and her expression gradually brightened.

"Babies, I've missed you so much."

My sister gently hugs the cotton candy and nods her head slowly. They had a happy time on this beautiful planet for the first time in a long time.

The time spent on the Puppy Star was very short, but it was a precious moment. When I awoke, I relived the memory with tears in my eyes. Then, in the early morning air, when the moon was still rising, he looked out the window and asked the gods.

"God, why is a dog's life so short? Why are you taking away my loved ones so quickly?"

Every time I asked, I received no answer. I looked up at the sky and had a deep conversation with myself.

"Aren't you the One who created the world? So why is there so much grief and separation? When you let go of your loved ones, the void feels so great. Luck and Hope were very precious to me. How can I give back the love and joy they gave me? I don't know why the love you have given me should end with such a painful parting."

I kept asking the gods.

"You said you know everything, didn't you? So, are you aware of the pain of this breakup? Do you know the sadness and emptiness I feel as they leave me?"

Even as I shared the pain and sorrow I felt deep inside, I felt a small comfort coming from somewhere.

"Perhaps, because their lives were shorter, they were more precious? Maybe it was because the time we spent together was so precious that those brief moments were even more brilliant."

I longed that one day my family would be able to see me there again. When I watch the Maltese mother-daughter "Spring Girl" on YouTube, I see the overlap between cotton candy and my family. I often remember them. When I see Dal-lae's cute and Bom-i's adorable appearance, I am reminded of how Hope and Luck used to run around the house and make their families laugh. When Bom-yi, the mother, lovingly cares for her daughter, Dal-lae, the moments when Hope took care of Lucky are gone. I feel happy and nostalgic that the innocent and mischievous actions are revived in the appearance of the mother and daughter in this video.

I began to let go of a little bit of that, day by day.

PAWSiA

3-1 to taste

I think I made too many mistakes while raising Hope. Looking back now, I think the way I was raised was a bit old-fashioned. If you look at YouTube or Instagram these days, dogs seem to be really happy. When I see that there are so many services for dogs, I feel sorry that I can't do it.

Hope didn't change her leash to a harness until later, and it didn't allow her to socialize with other dogs. I felt like I was becoming more and more introverted.

Also, the floor was slippery, so I think I often fell down. Time passed, and I put a pad on it, but it was too late because it was my first time. Still, I helped my second child a lot, but I think I raised him without knowing too much about dogs. I'm so sorry about that.

Hope, I never took you to a dog pension. Every time I saw the dogs running around in a spacious pension with mountains and rivers enjoying nature, my heart ached. I wish you had gone to such a good place.

Nowadays, puppies are encouraged to develop social skills and have fun with a variety of games. Just imagining you going to a puppy kindergarten, meeting new friends, and playing a variety of games fills me with a sense of regret. It hurts so much that I didn't give you such an opportunity. I left you alone, and how lonely you must have been during that time.

Recently, there are many different services for dogs. There is a dog spa, dog yoga, and even a café for dogs. I have never been able to provide you with such a service. When I imagine you relaxing in a spa massage or stretching in a dog-friendly yoga class, I feel like I've been a caregiver who wasn't good enough.

Hopeful, lucky. I'm so sorry. I don't think I took better care of you. I was just happy to spend time with you, but I regret that I couldn't do more for you. Now I just want you to be happy on the other side of the rainbow bridge.

Lucky man, I'm so sorry I couldn't visit you more often. I'd visit him several times a day. If I had, I would have been able to be loved and live a little longer...And I think the hospital was so cramped and stuffy. Even the sky outside the window looked stuffy. Even though you were in so much pain, I think we just watched helplessly. I'm so sorry.

But even though you were in so much pain, you greeted us with a gentle wagging of your tail. At that moment, my heart felt like it was going to break. Because I knew you didn't lose your love for us even in the midst of your pain.

'Lucky, you won't be in pain anymore.

Now relax'.

When I have time, I often go to shelters for stray dogs. In the wild, it's hard to understand why this is the way it is in a world where people have to eat each other to sustain life. When we see the cruel act of the strong preying on the weak, we wonder what kind of providence God really is. If there were energy resonance in this world, how beautiful and peaceful it would be. Also, how wonderful it would be if we could coexist harmoniously without harming each other. However, this is only a mere ideal, and in reality, good and evil, creation and destruction always coexist. We may not be able to fully comprehend the duality of God, but we begin to realize its depth.

Animals are God's creations and our precious family. The love and loyalty they show is a purity that is hard to find in relationships. The pain of stray dogs is a sad reality that stems from human irresponsibility. They were once someone's precious family members, but they are abandoned for various reasons and live in pain. When you look at the puppies who spend their days in the shelter, you can see how much sadness and loneliness they go through. They endure each day in the cold cage, waiting for a love that will never return.

"Hey kids, it's sausage bread! Come on~ Let's eat together!"

The puppies happily run up and circle around me. Their fluffy fur and swaying tails make me smile.

However, I don't have a rope hanging from my arms. I don't feel the weight and movement that I'm used to.

Cotton candy, I'm so sorry. I know how much you loved to go for walks, but I didn't take you out enough because I was busy. On the way to work, and when I get home, I think of the paths I walked with you.

Hope, lucky ones, I miss you running around on your walks, wondering at the sound of your footsteps and the little things. Why didn't I walk with you more then? Why haven't I seen you running excitedly, smelling everywhere and happy more often?

How beautiful was the world in your eyes? I think I've been so busy with my daily life that I've missed out on the little happiness you feel. Sorry, babies. I miss the feeling of pulling the rope taut every time I go for a walk. If I could go back now, I'd like to spend more time with you. I want to wake up early in the morning, walk around the neighborhood, and play in your favorite park.

The puppies are still stomping their paws and hovering in front of me, but my arms are still empty. Soon, he rubs his nose and body against my leg in an attempt to get his attention, but every time he does, his heart aches. Just like the two cotton candy did. Their love left a sour and sweet taste on my lips. The taste melted into my memory like cotton candy.

3-2 Fragrance

I still don't know what love is. I don't know exactly what that word means, but I do feel that what the two princesses have given me is love.

"Love endures, love is meek, love is not envious, does not boast, is not proud...."

When I read these verses, I understand what the word love means. I think that's what the cotton candy showed.

Even when we made mistakes, you always waited patiently for us and looked at us with gentle eyes.

I still have vivid memories of that birthday party. I was so happy when my whole family got together, put on our hats, put on the festive spirit, and shouted "I love you."

You guys happily put on your hats and ran back and forth, having fun. Seeing that made my heart light up. It was so precious to have that moment when we all came together as one and made love.

I still remember the scene where we looked at each other and shouted, "I love you!" I can see Luck and Hope wagging their tails with joy and screaming along with us. I think your pure love has brought our whole family together.

I think I'm finally starting to understand what the word love means. And I want to tell the two angels who gave me that love, the sweet and sour cotton candy.

"I love you. The love you showed me touched my heart."

It was a love that seemed to last forever, but eventually the breakup came.

My dear, I loved you so much. From the pure look in your eyes, your adorable demeanor, and your endless love and loyalty, I could see the depth of the love I received. Even now, when I think of your warm body in these arms, my heart is touched. I was so happy when you fell asleep peacefully in my arms.

Whenever I touched your ear, I would gently wag my tail to express my joy.

When I tickle the tip of your nose, I remember how you snorted and enjoyed yourself. Each time, my heart was filled with joy.

Hope, you've always been by my side and believed in me. The warmth I felt when you sat on my lap, the serenity I felt as you stroked that soft fur, that was love. As the saying goes, "Love is not something that is given freely, but something that is done together", every moment I spend with you has been love for me.

Lucky you, you have always given me hope and courage. Every time you run toward me with your bright eyes and wagging tail, my heart fills with joy. As the saying goes, "Love is considering the happiness of the other person as your own happiness," your small happiness was a big happiness for me.

I think love is sometimes expressed in tears, sometimes in laughter. I realized with you the saying, "Love is not just about sharing joy, but also about sharing sorrow." When you were sick, the pain and tears I felt, that was also love.

What is love? I think the time I've spent with you has brought me one step closer to that answer.

As the saying goes, "Love is understanding and embracing everything," the love you gave me was understanding and embracing itself. The look in your eyes when you looked at me, the moments when you felt my touch, were the greatest gift to me.

Hopeful, lucky. I will never forget the love you gave me. Even though we are separated now, as the saying goes, "Love transcends space," I will continue to love you, waiting for the day when we will meet again.

'Babies, please know that I loved you so much.'

Pets leave us with a 'smell of memories'. This smell conveys the joy and happiness that we had together. As time passes and the grief subsides, we can't rub our faces against the warmth of the hair on our chests, but we can touch the ossuary and reminisce about the days we spent together. She prays to the departed puppies, hoping that one day she will be with them again.

'Cotton candy doesn't melt.'

Cotton candy is love. Its soft and light texture, its fluttering appearance, and its delicacy when it touches the hand evoke the feeling of love. The sweetness we feel every time we eat cotton candy is no different from the joy that love gives us. The freely changing cotton candy, which can also be made into a heart shape, is special. The sensation that the softness and sweetness of cotton candy gives us is like love sinking into our hearts.

As we take a bite of cotton candy, we savor the love one by one. It's as if we share our love with each other little by little and feel its preciousness. Sometimes, however, we reflect on whether we've swallowed the sweetness too quickly and if we haven't savored enough of the moments of love. When you're done eating the cotton candy, all that's left is the sweet reverberation in your hands.

Love is no different. Even after we have eaten up all love, the reverberations of that love are still imprinted in our hearts. That love will never melt, it will abide forever.

3-3 Forever

Good luck and hope, thank you so much. Thank you so much for always being by my side since my school days.

Lucky for you, you've always been a bright light in my life. As the saying goes, "Gratitude is an expression of love that sinks deep into the heart," and I am infinitely grateful to you. The unconditional love you gave me has enriched my life. As the saying goes, "Gratitude is the key to happiness," the time I spent with you was a great happiness for me.

Hope, you've always supported me.

As the saying goes, "Gratitude is the best way to show love," there are so many ways to show how grateful I am to you. The sense of security and serenity I felt every time you were by my side made my life more meaningful.

As the saying goes, "Gratitude deepens our relationships with the people we love," and my relationship with you has always been special to me.

As the saying goes, "Gratitude starts with small things", every little moment I spent with you was precious. Your warm eyes and gentle touch have been a great comfort to me.

As the saying goes, "Gratitude heals our souls," you were a great healer to me.

And whenever I've been hurt and hurt by humans, you've always embraced me warmly.

Sometimes, I neglected you because of my girlfriend, my studies, my social life, etc., but you all understood me and gave me infinite love. Every time I look back on the most difficult moments of my life, I am reminded of how much strength your presence has given me.

I had a hard time at the time. And when I said that, my friends, colleagues, and even my girlfriend would turn me away. They just avoided me because it was a nuisance, and left me.

Especially that day, when I came home with my decision to leave, you were already waiting at my door before I opened it. The moment I hugged your warm body, it was as if the heavy stone in my chest was lightened a little. As soon as I entered the living room, tears welled up in my eyes, and in those tears were all despair and loneliness. As I slumped down on the couch and covered my head, he quietly came back to my side.

He stared at me, then slowly approached me and gently licked the back of my hand. The moment that little tongue brushed my hand, the tears I had been holding back burst out.

It was like saying, "It's okay, I'm here." And for a while, without saying a word, she was there for me, as if she knew how hard it was.

A short time later, another day, my girlfriend and I broke off our marriage. It was the same when I came home. As soon as you saw me, you jumped up and comforted me with your little body.

You don't know how comforting your unconditional love and devotion have been. If it hadn't been for you at that time, I might have really collapsed.

Cotton candy. Even if the shape changes, its stickiness and sweetness will remain in our hands and hearts, and will connect us forever.

Realizing the meaning of true love through parting. I felt a sense of fullness in the emptiness. The essence of that love blossomed within me. Without that love, I wouldn't be who I am today. We need to get rid of our selfish selves and practice a more pure love as they showed. And so that that this love can be transmitted to all living beings in the world.

\<Cotton candy never melted\>

Unlike humans, animals live with an appreciation and understanding of each other's differences. He treated us with pure love and loyalty. Unfortunately, we often use the phrase "worse than a dog" to demean someone. However, compared to dogs who are infinitely loving and loyal, we don't know how many flaws humans have. They are different from the front, they are treacherous, they are selfish, and they are naïve.

The proverb "When a hen crows, the house is ruined" has also been changed to "If you listen to a woman, even a loaf of bread will come out when you sleep." We need to rethink that as well.

The Republic of Korea still has a long way to go. There is an abundance of abandoned abandoned animals, and some veterinarians and lucrative pet companies are busy treating animals as commodities and making profits. And some do not hesitate to exploit and abuse weak animals.

No matter how self-aware human beings are, they are beings under the providence of nature. For society to truly develop, it needs to be protected and considerate of the weak. That is the way to respect and understand each other.

Even at this moment of writing, I felt the softness and warmth of the fur.

My beloved cotton candy

Maltese Hope is sour cotton candy, Lucky is sweet cotton candy. Sweet and sour cotton candy doesn't melt.

The sweet and sour scent took me back to my childhood memories. Every time I think of them, I feel their special scent again.

The sweetness made me happy. Their warmth and innocence sweetened my heart. Every time their little tongue licked their faces, they could taste the love.

The softness of the cotton candy is nostalgic as their warm body temperature and fur remain on their fingertips.

The colorful cotton candy was pleasing to the eye. The white fur covered with three black beans, the pinkish belly, and the jelly on the soles of the feet gave the viewer a deadly cuteness.

Rustling cotton candy whispered in his ear. The sound of their footsteps brought a small blessing to everyday life.

The cotton candy melts in your mouth quickly, but the sweet and sour memory is always remembered. Likewise, their love and memories do not melt in the heart. They are still alive and dancing in my senses.

If you take a leisurely walk in front of your house, you'll come across a lot of dogs. When you look at their pure eyes and happy faces, you can't help but smile.

Today I was on my way down to my old house to do some youth volunteer work. Even though they have moved, I still come here from time to time to feel their traces. Their smell permeating the wallpaper, the bitten corners of their babies, and the empty beds of their babies...

Their breath in this room touches me. I'm grateful for the traces left here.

Having a dog comes with a lot of responsibility, but the joy and love she gets is irreplaceable. And I would like to express my gratitude to readers who have dogs. Their love will enrich your home and your life, and we live in remembrance of that love. Not only dogs, but all pets remind us of the value of unchanging love.

If there was a God, he might have sent them as a gift to a world mired in materialism, selfishness, and humanism. Meeting them was the greatest hope and good fortune in my bleak life. If I ever ascend to their stars, I want to share those moments of love with them once again.

The cotton candy didn't melt.

My tears and runny nose were covered and dripped, but they hadn't melted yet.

Cotton candy never melted.